"Does This Fig Leaf Make Me Look Fat?"

Helping women escape the age-old trap of looking for joy in all the wrong places...

Merry Taylor
with
Linda Sloan

Copyright © 2011 by Merry Taylor and Linda Sloan

Does This Fig Leaf Make Me Look Fat?
A Guide revealing the 5 best ways to live life with joy and purpose
by Merry Taylor and Linda Sloan

Printed in the United States of America

ISBN 9781619044111

All rights reserved solely by the author. The author guarantees all contents are original and do not infringe upon the legal rights of any other person or work. No part of this book may be reproduced in any form without the permission of the author. The views expressed in this book are not necessarily those of the publisher.

Unless otherwise indicated, Bible quotations are taken from The Life Application Study Bible, New International Version. Copyright © 1991 by Tyndale House Publishers and Zondervan Publishing House.

Illustrations by Rosemary Gray

www.xulonpress.com

Acknowledgements

It is with great appreciation that we acknowledge the writers of the stories, poems and experiences shared in this book. For privacy purposes, we have included only the first names of those who gave us permission to use their names. We made every attempt to give proper credit to authors of quotes and excerpts from books, magazines and movies.

We especially thank Rosemary Gray, Jessie Smith and Brandy Foxe for sharing their artistic gifts, as well as Amelia Smith, who patiently read and reread the manuscript in its early stages.

A very special "thank you" goes to our families, who have provided a WEALTH of examples for us to use to illustrate life's fears, frustrations, failures, triumphs and joys.

Merry and Linda

Table of Contents

Introduction: I Can't Handle All These Problems, Please Pass the Twinkies! ix

Chapter 1   Don't Look Now, but Your Attitude Is Showing 13

(Attitude)

What is Attitude? 13
Where to Start? 16
Seven Ways to Change Attitude 18
Positive Attitude Stories 37

Chapter 2   Laughter: Joy in the Middle of Junk 49

(Laughter and Humor)

Do We Laugh Because We're Happy or
Are We Happy Because We Laugh? 49
How Do We Find Laughter and Humor? 58
Laughter Lightens and Brightens Our Days 67
Pulling Smiles from the Memory Banks 73
Laughter Stories 77

**Chapter 3 Feeling Like a Raggedy Ann in a
Barbie World** 96

(Self-Esteem and Purpose)

This Thing Called Self-Esteem 96
Where Do We Get Our Self-Esteem? 97
Improving Self-Esteem 102
Growing in Faith, Esteem and Purpose 123
Self-Esteem Stories 127

**Chapter 4 And Adam Said, "Eve Honey,
Have You Seen My Rib?"** 144

(Male/Female Communication)

News Flash—Men and Women Are Different 144
What Men and Women Say—and What They Mean 152
Building Better Communication—
Where to Turn First 155
Communication and Relationship Stories 169

**Chapter 5 Fill'er Up, Lord There's a
Hole in My Heart Where Hope Used to Be** 184

(Faith)

Life Can Be Tough 184
Hope—A Gift From God 186
Faith and Hope Stories 191

**Chapter 6 Put on That Red Dress... and
Go to the Party** 212

(Really *Living* Your Life)

INTRODUCTION

I Can't Handle All These Problems, Please Pass the Twinkies

I'm mad. I'm worried. I'm tired. I'm bored. Nobody understands me. I'm disappointed. I'm overworked and underappreciated...I'm hungry! Admit it. Sometimes when life becomes too stressful and overwhelming, chocolate just seems to jump out of the wrapper and into your mouth. That may not sound very intelligent, professional or faith-based, but it does sound *human*, and many women can identify with turning to chocolate for stress relief. The problem with always reaching for food is that what usually follows is weight gain and plummeting self-esteem. How many of us have ever said, "Does this dress make me look fat?" Probably Eve was doing the same thing with her fig leaf! Many women, since the time of Eve, have looked for joy and affirmation in all the wrong places. We put pressure on ourselves and try to be all things to all people. Think about it. How often do we hear a man say, "Do these pants make me look fat?"

When tough times hit—and they do for everybody at some point—each person *chooses* a way to get through them. These choices are called coping skills. I compare our coping skills to the root systems of trees. Small storms come along and the trees that sway and give during the storm do pretty well, with just a few limbs and leaves broken off. But let a major storm, like a hurricane, arrive and even some of the huge trees are uprooted. If we look at their exposed root systems, we will see that they are very shallow, with nothing to ground them. The trees that make it through these storms are the ones that have deep, wide root systems that spread out and anchor the trees.

We know people who are like both kinds of trees. There are those who seem to live charmed lives with very few problems, and yet all they do is complain. Nothing is ever right and they're totally stressed out. These are the people you learn not to ask how they are doing. If you do, their eyes light up and they follow you down the hall complaining... forever! On the flip side are those about whom you're thinking, "What else can happen to this poor person?" Yet that individual is positive, joyful and lives life to the fullest. This doesn't happen by accident. What makes the difference? It's the root system... how that person is grounded. I once rode by a church and this saying was out front—*Lives that are rooted in Christ are not uprooted*. When God is the center of our lives, fears diminish.

Looking back at what has helped me the most through life's trials, and from teaching stress management workshops across the country, I finally realized that there really are some areas that provide a foundation and direction for handling life's challenges. Between us, Linda and I have over 60 years of experience in helping people manage stress. Through the years when we asked women what helped them the most to live life with joy and purpose, five ways were shared over and over.

This book takes a practical and humorous look at how faith, our relationship with God, and those five ways can help us find joy and purpose, live above circumstances, and manage stress in constructive ways.

It was written *by* women *for* women, to *encourage* women to use what Linda and I, and thousands of other women, believe to be life's foundations or root systems: *positive attitude, laughter, self-esteem and purpose, male/female communication* and most important of them all—*faith and prayer*. Real-life inspirational stories, from many women and men, are included. We invite you to smile, laugh, and maybe even shed a tear or two from a story or chapter that touches you. Enjoy!

Merry and Linda

CHAPTER ONE

Don't Look Now, But Your Attitude Is Showing
(Attitude)

"All the days of the oppressed are wretched, but the cheerful heart has a continual feast."
Proverbs 15:15

"For there is nothing good or bad, but thinking makes it so."
Shakespeare

What is Attitude?

The best way to start thinking about this thing called attitude is to take yourself through a typical day, starting from the time you wake up in the morning until the time you drop into bed at night. Try to recall everything that happens in that time frame that influences your attitude. Include people, thoughts, events, and situations that you encounter throughout the day.

INFLUENCES AT WORK   INFLUENCES AT HOME
_____
_____
_____
_____
_____

Now go back over both lists and place a check by each thing you wrote that influences your attitude in a positive way. Don't check items that could go either way. Check only those items that you were thinking *positively* about as you wrote them. Next, go back and check all the items that are *directly* and *totally* under your control.

If you're like most people doing this exercise, you haven't checked many items. It's important to note that the assignment read "...recall everything that happens...that influences your attitude." It did not read, "List everything that happens to you that puts you in a bad mood." Most of us tend to focus on the negative things that come along during the day. We also tend to focus on things over which we have little or no control. Frequently mentioned items include co-workers, kids' attitudes, the weather, the boss, my spouse, the telephone ringing at work, etc. The important message here is this: If we focus on the negative and allow our attitudes to be jerked around by actions and situations we can't control, we will find ourselves on a never-ending emotional roller coaster.

Attitude is how an individual sees, feels or perceives something. It is very personal. If you lined up one hundred people and asked them to look at the same picture, you might get one hundred different opinions or attitudes about that one picture. An attitude is basically what we say to ourselves in our own minds. And if *we say something to ourselves long enough, we will eventually believe it!*

7/11/2012 3:16 PM   Sales Receipt #783
Store: 1

Mae's on Main

121 East Main Street
Lexington, SC 29072
803-359-4545
MaesofLexington@gmail.com
WWW.MAESOFLEXINGTON.COM

Item Name	Qty	Price	Ext Price
Book	1	$10.00	$10.00 T
		Subtotal	$10.00
Local Sales Tax		7 % Tax	+ $0.70
		RECEIPT TOTAL:	**$10.70**

Amount Tendered: $11.00
Change Given: $0.30

Cash $11.00

Refunds & exchanges in 5 days.
No Refund on Sale Items Please.   Thanks
for shopping with us!

783

Our attitudes color our personalities and outlooks. Philippians 4:8 helped Paul when he faced prison. *"Finally, brothers, whatever is true, whatever is noble, whatever is right, whatever is pure, whatever is lovely, whatever is admirable—if anything is excellent or praiseworthy—think about such things."* The point is that few people want pain and problems. A positive attitude can help us get through those tough times and, sometimes, those tough times can even become blessings. If I didn't believe that one door closes as another door opens, I probably would have crawled into a hole by now and died. But I will admit that sometimes when that door is being slammed over and over in my face, it can be very difficult to believe another door is opening. Once during a rough time in my life, someone said to me, "I know it's bad right now, but it will build character." At that moment what I *wanted* to respond with was, "Well, I have enough ##*## character, thank you very much!!"

A positive attitude can be a powerful stress management technique, if we remember that we cannot control others, we cannot control many situations that life presents, but we *can* control how we *react* to and learn to *handle* the cards we're dealt.

Many people find themselves literally paralyzed by circumstances they can do nothing about. One particular situation stands out in my mind. Craig was referred to me by his physician for some stress management coaching, because he let things really "get" to him and developed stress-related health problems. He was telling me all that was going on and then said to me, "If I could just get rid of all these problems, then I could have a good attitude and enjoy life." Craig was an intelligent man, but he just didn't get it. If we wait on everything to be perfect, with no problems, before we can have positive attitudes and enjoy life, then *we're in for a long wait!* There will always be problems. So the question becomes, *How can we enjoy life and have a positive attitude in spite of problems?* This chapter is devoted to teaching the building blocks of a better attitude: realistic and practical ways to control the only thing we can...OURSELVES!

> *"A woman is like a tea bag: you never know how strong she is until she gets in hot water."*
>
> *Nancy Reagan*

> *"No pessimist ever discovered the secret of the stars, or sailed to an uncharted land, or opened a new doorway for the human spirit."*
>
> *Helen Keller*

Where to Start?

To work on our attitudes, we need to have starting points. If someone said to me, "I always have a positive attitude and am never down or negative," my first thought would be—*liar, liar, pants on fire*! Even the most positive person has times when she feels low and weak. Sometimes life can be so overwhelming we just feel like we're hanging on by a thread. The challenge is how to pull ourselves out of those bad moods or deep pits and start over again. Someone once said to me, "Why go to a motivational program or read something motivational? It doesn't last." Well, duh, that's the whole point of motivation. Life is not constantly three steps forward and none back. Often it's one forward and, slam, four back. That's where motivation and attitude come in. We refuel and start forward again.

I've frequently heard people say, "Well, that's not fair," or "Life's not fair." (maybe even thought or said it myself a *few* times!) And you know what? They are exactly right... life is not fair! Barbara Johnson, in her book, *Splashes of Joy in the Cesspools of Life*, expresses it well with this comment:

"The rain falls on the just and also the unjust, but chiefly on the just, because the unjust steals the just's umbrella." [1]

At this time in your life, how would you rate your attitude? On a scale from 1 to 10, with 1 being lousy and 10 being great, rate your attitude right now. Then briefly explain in the space that follows why you gave yourself that number.

<u>WHY?</u>

_____
_____
_____
_____

I'm one of the first to admit that having, developing or keeping a positive attitude is often difficult. My husband sometimes irritates me because he is so optimistic and positive. Now don't get me wrong, I'm very glad he is that way. But, to be honest, I guess I'm jealous because I have to work so *hard* at being positive.

> *"I have not failed. I've just found 10,000 ways that won't work."*
> Thomas Edison

There are many misconceptions about this thing called attitude. Go to any local bookstore and you'll find at least twenty or thirty books telling you how important it is to have a positive attitude, but few of them give you the building blocks needed to successfully accomplish a change. There are basically three things that must happen for change to be successful:

1. **SEE THE NEED**—how can you change something that you are not even aware you are doing?

2. **WANT TO CHANGE**—buy into the benefits of the change

3. **JUST DO IT**—not next week, not next month—get started now

Seven Ways to Change Attitude
Once you've committed to making a positive change in your attitude, consider using these seven ways to get you started:

Prayer
Thought stopping
Styles of thinking
Wellness connection
Back to basics
The flip-flop technique
Horse blinders

PRAYER
Faith with prayer is the one constant and most powerful thing we have. It is where we need to start and end when trying to change our attitudes. None of the other techniques will work well if we do not have a strong faith in God and pray.

My minister's sermon one Sunday had the title "Despair Repair." He talked about the pain and hurt all human beings endure, from his own open-heart surgeries to deaths in his family. As I sat and listened, I thought about a forty-four-year-old friend of mine who is dying of cancer and has a five-year-old daughter. So many things happen that we just do not understand. I've heard many people say, "It's just not fair that so and so has cancer or is ill." And I would agree.

But we all know that life is *not* fair. We need to embrace the attitude that God has a plan and ask Him to show us how to obey, accept and learn from it.

I know God had a plan for me concerning children. When I remarried, I already had one child and my husband had three, but we knew we had enough love for another child. I got pregnant right away, but lost the baby. After trying unsuccessfully to have another child, we decided to adopt. Since I was already forty-one years old, we decided to begin the process of private adoption through a physician.

Several months later Amy, my nine-year-old stepdaughter, had a serious accident. She suffered severe head injuries, lapsed into a coma, and was not expected to live. My husband's other two children temporarily moved in with us, my son was living at home, and we were both working full time. Needless to say, with everything going on, the adoption never entered my mind. About six weeks went by. One day my physician called and said a woman was giving up her baby for adoption after it was born (due in three months), and asked if we wanted the child. We had one week to make a decision. Looking back now, I realize more than ever how much God played a role in our attitude and decision-making concerning the adoption. BECAUSE, NO NORMAL FULL-TIME WORKING COUPLE WOULD EVER IN A MILLION YEARS THINK ABOUT ADOPTING A BABY WITH ONE CHILD IN INTENSIVE CARE IN A COMA AND THREE OTHER CHILDREN LIVING AT HOME! But *we* did. Ashley and I prayed and our answer was immediate. We just *knew* that was what we were supposed to do. We told no one except our children and my mother. Her first response was, "Are you out of your mind?"

Amy lived. Weeks went by and she gradually started coming out of her coma. One day I was in my office at work when the phone rang. It was the adoption attorney telling me our baby was here. She was born about three or four weeks early. I had to call a friend I was meeting for lunch and tell her I couldn't make lunch because I'd just had a baby! Then I walked into my boss's office and told him I needed a week off, since my baby was coming home the next day. You can imagine the shock to everyone and us, too. We had no bed, food or clothes—nothing!

Baby Allison came home, Amy eventually got out of the hospital, and we lived through some interesting, and I *mean* interesting, times. But never once did my husband and I question our decision about adopting Allison. We just *knew* that was what we were supposed to do. God does His work, and at the time we may not understand, but He has a plan. Now Ashley and I understand God *chose* us to have Allison instead of our choosing her. She has had many health and emotional challenges, and when I start feeling negative and my attitude needs an adjustment, I just pray and ask God to give me strength to carry out what He chose for us. Everything is for a reason, and I feel we were chosen to help give a child that has many problems a chance at life.

Another time when prayer truly helped change my attitude was when my Mother died. I felt so alone. Several days after the funeral I went to her home to start the cleaning-out process. As I walked up the steps to her front door, my attitude could best be described as dread and sorrow, because the house would feel so empty without her. In the kitchen, lying in a small plate that collected odds and ends, was a little piece of paper that I hadn't noticed the last time I was there. Curious, I picked it up and read it. It was this poem:

Do not stand at my grave and weep;
I am not there. I do not sleep.

I am a thousand winds that blow;
I am the diamond glints on snow,

I am the sunlight on ripened grain;
I am the gentle autumn's rain.

When you awaken in the morning's hush,
I am the swift uplifting rush
Of quiet birds in circled flight.
I am the soft star that shines at night.

Do not stand at my grave and cry.
I am not there; I did not die.[2]

By Mary E. Frye

Then I started to cry. Not from grief, but from the comfort that God is love and that love is all around us, as was my Mother's love at that very moment.

After we pray, then all the other attitude-changing techniques take on the proper perspective. A poet said it well:

One ship sails east
One ship sails west
Regardless of how the winds blow.
It is the set of the sail
And not the gale
That determines the way we go.[3]

By Ella Wheeler Wilcox

THOUGHT STOPPING (TAPE PLAYER TECHNIQUE)

My children used to play this stuff they called music and I called noise. They would leave their tape players blaring, even after they had left their rooms. I could have ranted and raved until I was blue in the face, but unless I did something, the "music" would continue to play. If I did not want to listen to it or play that tape anymore, it would be necessary for me to hit the stop button. Sweet relief would come immediately...but only temporarily. If I left in the same tape, the same "music" would continue the next time I hit play. I could try to jam my favorite tape into the slot, but it wouldn't work with the old tape still in there. Our brains work the same way. We cannot change our thought patterns without first stopping the old negative thoughts. Simply breaking the connection is not enough. We have to remove the old tapes from our thinking by hitting the eject button immediately after the stop button. This is the only way to remove the thoughts that keep us from building positive attitudes. For example, if we're playing tapes like, "If I make a mistake, I'm a failure," or "I'm not smart enough," or "I can never learn to do that," then those tapes or thoughts can become very self-defeating. The only way to move toward positive tapes or positive attitudes is to first stop the thoughts and then eject them.

STYLES OF THINKING (TAPE SELECTION)

If we want to work on having more positive attitudes, we have to work on our choice of thoughts or what tape we choose to play in our minds. The new tape must be realistic, though, because we could never buy into or believe the new tape, if it is totally out of our belief or value system. For example, a person working in customer service that is "cussed out" by a customer would have great difficulty changing her tape from *I hate this* to *Oh, this feels so good. I just love being cussed out. Please do that again.* However, she might work on saying this to herself, *The customer is not angry at me, he's upset that no one has helped him and I'm not going to take it personally.* You might be thinking—*oh, sure, that would be the first thought to pop into my head*! Of course, it probably wouldn't. That's because most of us have become so accustomed to reacting defensively that we do it out of habit. Well, the only way to change a habit is to consciously choose to do things differently (change the tape) and practice the new technique (play the new tape over and over).

Linda shares the following story about how she used thought-stopping and changing her style of thinking to better handle the challenges of her children's teenage years:

When our oldest son was a small boy, he would delight in bringing me beautiful weeds plucked fresh from our yard. I'd ooh and aah over them and put them in a juice glass on the window sill for all to admire. When he would go out of town with a friend's family, he'd bring me a gift that he picked out and paid for himself. My heart would swell!

Then he turned 13—and I became convinced that we might need the services of an exorcist! That sweet boy turned into a mumbling, eye-rolling, shoulder-shrugging, disagreeable creature that I hardly recognized. Having grown up in a home with two sisters and no brothers, I had never experienced life with a teenage boy first-hand. Things got to the point that I began to dread having any sort of discussion with him. I'm not proud of what I am about to tell you, but it is true. The bus bringing my son home from Hand Middle School rolled into our neighborhood at 4pm every day. I can still see myself working at the kitchen sink, looking out the window to the spot where the bus would stop, checking my watch and moaning to myself, 'Well, it's almost time. Here we go again. He'll be getting off the bus soon and I'm dreading it. I know exactly what's going to happen. He won't be in here 3 minutes before we get into an argument about something.'

Sure enough, we were usually arguing soon after his arrival. What I came to realize was that it wasn't all his fault. What I said to myself before he arrived set the tone for the look on my face and the tone in my voice before he ever walked through the door! So, I decided to change my style of thinking. Instead of reviewing all the negatives in our relationship before he arrived, I decided to try to be more positive. I could have said to myself, 'I know today will be different. I'll bet he's changed. I love it when he acts like that!' Each of those statements would have set me up for further disappointment. Instead, I tried telling myself true statements that changed the way I prepared myself for his arrival. 'He's 13 years old. His hormones are raging. He's facing peer pressure that I can't even imagine at school. This too shall pass. I'm not going to let the roller coaster emotions of a teenager keep me from being myself and greeting him with love and a smile. If he's disrespectful, I'll deal with it; but I'll start out by being positive myself.' The amazing thing was that, even when he lost his temper, what I said to myself before he arrived left me better able to keep my cool, handle his moods and still function as a reasonably sane mom!

We can choose the way we want to look at something. We have a choice. A woman in one of my classes once said to me, "Your first thought is an impulse, and you don't have much control over it. But your second thought can and *ought* to be controlled. Guess on which one most of us open our mouths?"

Look at the following self-talks. First read the negative, or out-of-control self-talks, and then look at the positive or in-control self-talks:

NEGATIVE: I'm too old to learn to work a computer.
POSITIVE: The tech school offers computer classes for all ages and skill levels.

NEGATIVE: Why bother to lose weight? I'll just gain it back.
POSITIVE: This time I'll lose slowly and change slowly.

This idea that attitude is a choice, no matter what the situation, once again really hit home after Amy, my stepdaughter, got out of the hospital. She was in a wheelchair and had a long road to recovery in front of her. Allison, the baby, had breathing problems and was on an apnea monitor that would sound an alarm if her breathing stopped or if the connection came loose. The alarm blared several times a night, so I rarely got more than a couple of hours' sleep without being interrupted by screams and buzzers. I can remember breaking down one night, falling into a big time pity-party and crying uncontrollably saying, "Nothing will ever be the same. I'll never be happy again." My husband patiently let me cry and then said something to me I have never forgotten. He said, "I don't know what will happen to Amy or Allison, only God knows that. However, I do know one thing. No matter what, I will *choose* to be happy and positive." And he did. I realized then that I was focusing and thinking on only negative thoughts.

Joy and peace do not depend on outside events. These are determined more from how we *choose* to handle life's situations. Have you ever known someone to whom life has been very unfair, enduring heartache after heartache? Yet this person is positive, optimistic and cheerful most of the time. That doesn't happen by accident. It takes effort and work to develop a positive attitude, and the belief that as one door closes, another door opens. First we pray, which is talking to God, and then we talk to ourselves (self-talks).

A minister was once referred for stress management coaching because his stress level had increased to the point that it was contributing to health problems. I explained to him the thought stopping and styles of thinking techniques and he said to me, "Do you know that what you just taught me is in the Bible?" As I gave him a puzzled look, he recounted Jesus' story in Matthew 12: 43-45, about a man who was demon-possessed. Jesus came along and cast the demon out of this man, but because the man was too lazy to take the time and energy to try to put good thoughts back in, seven demons rushed in to take the place of the one. This still applies today, doesn't it, as we struggle to overcome the "demons" of stress, worry and anxiety?

A woman in a class told me she was molested by an uncle when she was a young girl, and for years carried around bitterness and hatred. Realizing that her negative thoughts were starting to consume her, she worked on "letting go" of them and replacing them with thoughts of forgiveness. She told me that it took lots of prayer and lots of positive self-talks to be able to move on.

> *"For if you forgive men when they sin against you, your heavenly Father will also forgive you. But if you do not forgive men their sins, your Father will not forgive your sins."*
>
> Matthew 6:14-15

WELLNESS CONNECTION

Mind, body and spirit are all connected. One very definitely affects the other. If we want to improve our attitudes, then we have to look at this connection and deal with all three areas. For example, when we are exhausted, physically or mentally, it clouds the way we view situations. Everything looks darker and gloomier, and it's difficult to see situations in an objective way.

Have you ever had a time when you just felt "yucky," snippy or negative, and then *forced* yourself to go for a long, brisk walk? When you came dragging back with your tongue hanging out, the problem or situation hadn't changed, but your perspective surely had. It's so ironic that, in the area of exercise, the old saying—*When you need it the most is when you feel like doing it the least*—is so true. When we're tired, stressed and negative, many people often say exercise is the last thing they want to do. However, if we can just make ourselves do some form of exercise—walk, swim, bike—we almost always feel better, more positive and more energetic. Here's a little story about the importance of physical fitness:

> *A client called upon his wellness-oriented physician and exclaimed: "Doctor, you must help me. My self-concept has deteriorated, I'm overweight, my energy level is low, and I can't sleep nights. Worst of all, my wife says I'm unbearable, and doesn't want me around the house anymore. What's wrong?" Without hesitating, the insightful physician said: "I know what your problem is: you are physically unfit. Here's what I want you to do. Run ten miles daily for the next 15 days." Immediately, the client responded: "Doctor, that makes sense. I'll do it." And 15 days later, he called the physician and reported that he did as recommended, and the results were wonderful. That is, his self-concept was terrific, he had lost weight, had high energy levels, and slept soundly at night. "Fine, fine," said the physician, "but tell me, how are you getting along with your wife?" "How the #*# should I know?" the man replied. "She's 150 miles away."*[4]

Of course, this story is not true, but it does show the benefits of exercise. If we're looking for ways to change attitudes, taking care of ourselves should be high on our lists. Wellness-oriented people make positive, conscious decisions about lifestyles, and these decisions affect attitudes and how we handle stress.

BACK TO BASICS

Too often we allow our lives to become so complicated and filled with problem-producing details that it becomes difficult to keep a positive attitude and focus on what is really important.

A woman in one of my classes shared the story of her flowers. One summer she planted many flowerbeds. Then she filled dozens of pots with plants that had to be watered daily. At first she said it was rewarding. But eventually it got to the point where she realized all she was doing was complaining about the work involved with the flowers. There was no joy left or time to do other things important to her. Instead of having a positive attitude, it became increasingly negative. Time to think—*back to basics. What do I really want?*

Sometimes it takes a "teachable moment," something life-changing, in order to get our attention. In 1989 hurricane Hugo hit near Charleston, SC. After the severe storm, rescue teams went in to help the devastated areas. Also, teams from mental health arrived to offer counseling and emotional assistance. A volunteer told me this story:

Each counselor had a list of questions to ask individuals to determine who might need follow-up. One woman came in, started wringing her hands and saying, "All my antiques, everything was destroyed, all my things gone." When asked about her family she replied, *"Oh, my family is all right, but everything that matters to me is gone. All my beautiful things are gone."* This woman was flagged for follow-up counseling. It seemed that things were more important to her than people, and she was very negative and depressed.

Shortly afterwards a man walked in. The same questions were addressed to him and he shared his story.

"My house was severely damaged and most of my furniture was destroyed. You know I've lived here eight years and didn't even know any of my neighbors, because I was always too busy working. Now all the neighbors are emptying their freezers and we're cooking roasts, steaks and stuff on gas grills. We might be dirty, but we're sure eating well. I've seen my children more in the last week than I have in three months and I've actually talked to my wife. Aw, I never liked my old durn, tacky furniture anyway."

This man needed no follow-up. In fact, he probably grew stronger emotionally because of the crisis.

When crises happen in our lives, we do not stay the same. We either get *bitter* or *better*.

I think this poem, written by my cousin, expresses the right attitude about life:

Life
Grasp the light of each new day
Welcome it as you begin to pray.

When life seems no longer to offer reason,
And it matters not whatever the season.

You have life and you are still aware
You still have loved ones who really care,

Hold on to this life with all you possess,
Embrace it; hold it to your breast.

Find again the joy of the first flower of spring,
Of a snowflake or another sweet unimportant thing.

Seek the once enjoyed little pleasure,
Of a new book, a new poem or little treasures.

Fill your life with uplifting goals,
Pushing yourself as in days of old.
Begin a new endeavor, one thought beyond reach,
Give it your best, use the ole stubborn streak.

Don't waste a precious day, dreading the end,
Face your life head on with task in hand.

The quality of your life lies in your mind,
It can overcome fears of any kind.

What a gift your contentment can be,
For all who are hanging on your family tree!

Margie Tolly

FLIP-FLOP TECHNIQUE

Sometimes a negative, frustrating or even painful situation can seem less overwhelming if we can flip-flop our thought processes and find some humor in it. After my stepdaughter, Amy, went home from months in the hospital, she was strapped in a wheelchair and had very little control of her arms and coordination. Also, her eyes were crossed and her voice squeaked because of damage to her vocal cords. Amy would visit on weekends, but it was difficult for her and us.

Allison, our adopted infant daughter, was on an apnea monitor because of breathing problems. She had wires attached to a halter worn around her body, and lights on this monitor blinked on and off. If Allison quit breathing or the wires came loose, an alarm went off that rivaled a five-alarm fire. To be honest, there wasn't much fun or humor in our lives at this time. It was very easy for me to feel trapped and to focus only on all the negative things. After months of doing nothing but going to work and then coming home to deal with problems, one Saturday night we decided to go to the mall. So the three kids climbed in the van. Then we strapped in Amy and her wheelchair. Finally we put Allison in her car seat with her monitor blinking and off we went. When we arrived at the mall, everyone climbed out and walked into one of the stores. There was a long downhill slope that started from our store on one end and went the entire length of the mall to a store at the other end. I was glancing in a store window, and when I turned around, I noticed one of our sons standing behind Amy in her wheelchair and the other son standing behind Allison in her stroller. Just then one of them hollered, "I'll race you", and off they went. Amy was making garbled sounds of glee, arms flailing as her wheelchair was burning rubber. Allison's stroller was also moving out, with wires flapping everywhere and lights blinking. They went racing full speed down the long hill with our sons and Amy laughing, Allison squealing, and dozens of people *gaping*! What a sight! People were turning their heads with their mouths hanging open and staring. We truly looked like the Munsters or the Addams family on vintage television. At first I was embarrassed and horrified, and turned to see what my husband was doing about it. Leaning against a store window, he was doubled over laughing so hard he was crying. As I burst into laughter myself, it was then I realized that this was just what we all needed...to be able to laugh at our situation and ourselves.

HORSE BLINDERS

We own horses and enjoy riding. Sometimes, though, horses will "spook" when they are startled by noises or sudden movements. In parades people often put blinders on horses pulling wagons to help block out things that might scare or "spook" them. This way the horses will stay focused on things straight ahead.

Human beings also have a tendency to allow unimportant or trivial things to "spook" them. It's so easy to focus and dwell on the negatives in a situation, and on what we *don't* have instead of trying to look at what we *do* have.

I was in Georgia speaking at a convention where I had the pleasure of meeting a remarkable woman. She told me her husband had deserted the family when the children were very small. They had very little money and lived on a tight budget for years. When her children were about ten and eight, they began coming home from school talking about all the trips other families were taking. She stated that her children didn't complain or fuss, but she could tell they were feeling left out and sorry for themselves. Wanting to find a way to help her children stay positive, she came up with an idea. One afternoon she told them they were taking a trip and to decide where they wanted to go. It could be anywhere in the world. The children didn't understand, but each picked a favorite place or country. This woman then went to travel agencies and collected travel posters and decorations.

Several days passed. One afternoon after school, she told them that at suppertime they were going on a trip. Later that evening, as they entered the kitchen, the children gazed at walls that were covered in travel posters. Audiotapes, checked out from the local library, provided music popular in the country depicted on the travel posters. Decorations were everywhere and food was on the table. After dinner they played favorite games from that country.

Her children loved it. From then on each month they "visited" a new country. Refusing to allow her children to feel negative and sorry for what they didn't have, this remarkable woman created wonderful memories for her children and helped them focus on what they *did have*.

When I think of an example of the epitome of a positive attitude, one elderly gentleman comes to my mind. Several years ago I was driving down Interstate 95 on the way to a seminar at Hilton Head. As usual, I was by myself, so to pass the time I would listen to tapes and the radio. When that got boring I would people watch, because you see cars from all over the US on Interstate 95. I would set the cruise control and then watch as cars would pass. Most were going at a speed that enabled me to see their faces and read their license plates and bumper stickers. Out of nowhere a car flew past me going about ninety miles an hour. As it passed, I first thought it must be a teenager or young person driving, because it was going so fast.

I did a double take, because it was a man who appeared to be about ninety years old!

Because of the speed, I couldn't read his license plate, but no one could miss his bumper sticker. It started at one end of the rear bumper and wrapped all the way around to the other end. When I read it, I almost ran off the road laughing. Here was a ninety-year-old man, going about ninety miles an hour on the interstate, and sporting a bumper sticker that read: HONK, IF YOU'RE HORNY! Now that man had a positive attitude!

Once when I told that story in a class, a man raised his hand and said, "Well Merry, did you honk?" I replied, "Are you crazy?" Then he said, "Well, maybe that's why he's driving so fast. Maybe somebody honked at him!"

Positive Attitude Stories

These stories are true-life examples of ordinary people, just like you and me, who have dealt with adversity in life. They chose to face it with a positive attitude and approach. I hope you find these just as rewarding in reading them as we did in hearing them.

Attitude Counts

My name is Ron and for ten years I was a paramedic in a small town in South Carolina. One night we pulled a fifteen-year-old boy from under a car. He was covered in blood and in the dark I couldn't tell who he was. This was a "by the book" transport. After evaluation at our local hospital, we transported him to a trauma center and found out through his doctor that he had three spinal fractures and would never walk again or have kids. From time to time we would look in on him, when we had other trips to the trauma center.

About a year later, I got off work one morning, went home, kicked off my shoes, poured a cup of coffee and was relaxing a little. The doorbell rang and that boy walked in and said he just stopped by to thank me for what we did for him. He said the doctors told him if we had not taken the precautions we did and had the attitude about doing our job right, he would never have walked again. Plus, two years later he and his wife had a son.

R.W.

Tom

My little world was complete. The values and accomplishments I had set forth for my own personal achievements were looking up at me through the eyes of a newborn baby-my son. How happy my husband and I were that he was a boy. My mother, who was a patient in the same hospital at the time, was rolled down to see her first grandson and to make sure he was perfect. She was happy that he had all ten fingers and ten toes, a normal, healthy baby boy perfect in every way. Yes, perfect. My husband and I didn't realize at the time how truly perfect Tom was, and how he would be used to do perfect works in our lives.

When I held Tom in my arms, I felt a gnawing uneasiness I couldn't explain. For some strange reason I kept wondering if he would talk to me. I didn't have this feeling when I held his sister two years before. I dismissed these feelings, thinking I was confused and worried over my mother's illness. Mother died eight months later, still thinking she had a beautiful, healthy, normal grandson.

Looking back over my life, especially the earlier years, I can see how normal it was for me to have a child like Tom. I can remember being sent to the corner grocery store to purchase some product contained in a can. I would stand in front of the counter staring at the cans, always wanting to find the most damaged container. I knew when I returned home, I would have to listen again to the same lecture on why one should pick only the best cans. The fact remained; I was pulled to the bent ones. When I went to school, I chose Johnny to be my special friend. He was different from the rest of us. He always spoke in a strange way, usually stumbling over his words. His mannerisms were often exaggerated in movement, causing others to stare wide-eyed, but he was special to me. I would fight anyone who dared treat him with anything other than the respect he deserved. I wonder

Does This Fig Leaf Make Me Look Fat?

now why I had such a difficult time accepting the reality that my child, Tom, was also different.

My husband was so proud of his son and had great plans for his boy. Tom was going to play middle linebacker for the Clemson Tigers, wearing number 55. My future plans for Tom bounced back and forth. The awful feeling I had when he was put in my arms could always be pushed aside with visions of him entering medical school. The months and years passed, and my fears became more of a reality with each passing day. Tom wouldn't talk to me or anyone else. In fact, people frightened him. He was in his own world and no one could enter. His toys became his existence. Each toy had its specific place and to move one an eighth of an inch from the chosen position would cause continuous screams of terror.

My husband and I went from doctor to doctor to no avail. For three years we struggled through an unknown world of horror. We had so much faith in doctors. Surely they would write us a prescription that would cure Tom's illness. Our search for the answer ended when a doctor finally diagnosed our child as having early infantile autism. He said we could do nothing and added that it would have been better to have a retarded child because that type child at least showed love. The doctor continued by saying, "The only thing you can do is take him home and love him." He assured us Tom would eventually be confined to an institution, because all autistic people end up that way.

We reached the depth of depression, filled with anger. The child the professionals were referring to was our son, a beautiful, normal looking five-year-old with the biggest, brightest, blue eyes imaginable. How could this have happened? Other people had handicapped children, not us. At least we hoped not us. We were expecting another baby in a few months. Would this baby also be handicapped? I didn't even want to ask, because I didn't want to know the answer.

For the first time in my life, I was in utter panic in the world of reality.

I look back now and shudder. Those were dark days. Tom, burying himself deep within the clutter of inanimate objects, lived in a listless manner, oblivious to his surroundings and the world beyond. During this time, our family not only grew in number but in closeness. Meg was born, and all of us together sought ways to enter the world of Tom. Some of the programs proved to be exasperating and meaningless, but along the way something clicked. Tom began to experiment with language and laughter. Excitement permeated our family's morale. Tom was responding. He was breaking through the shell of silence and becoming a vital part of the family's being.

Eighteen years have passed, and I look into those big, blue eyes realizing how complete my world truly is... not what I had thought it would be, not what I had dreamed. Tom does not act like other boys his age, but the sunshine of his face and love in his heart spreads to all who know him. He will not play for the Clemson Tigers this year, but I bet he is their biggest fan. He will not be entering medical school four years from now, but he has astounded the medical field with his outstanding progress. Most of all, Tom will not be in an institution as the doctor of long ago predicted. He lives at home with us now. Someday he may share an apartment with some of his special friends, and I do mean special. For now, Tom goes to the Career Center and works part time for the Mets at Capital City Park, picking up trash. We're proud of what Tom is doing with his life and, more importantly, he is too.

My life did not turn out like I had planned, while sitting next to Johnny in Mrs. Griffin's second grade class or standing in the aisle of Steele's Grocery staring at bent cans; however, the fact remains that reality did set in as it does in some form to every human being. I know now that this

beautiful reality has touched me with a unique love, joy, and peace brought from above by a special messenger, Tom.
Mary Heath

Thank You, Cancer

On the last Advent Sunday, our priest talked about preparation—for Christmas and beyond—and closed with a request that each ask himself what in life he would change, if possible, and for what he would want to be forgiven. I immediately began to cry, thinking if only I could not have this cancer. Then a new thought came to mind. Even if I could make it never to have happened, I'm not sure I would, because then I would never know how much my family and friends and even strangers love me. They have given me a greater gift than life itself in their caring and support, and I would never have experienced that if not for my illness. Thank you, Cancer!

Sarah

My Mother—The Encourager

My Mother was a very special woman and I will be forever touched by her attitude about life. As she aged, became frailer and experienced many years of illness, I marveled at the consistent positive attitude that always prevailed as she dealt with health problems.

Mother never complained about how she felt and you had to specifically ask her to find out how she was feeling. On most days I knew Mother was not feeling well, and it would have been so easy for her to answer in detail how terrible she felt and seek pity from the family. If indeed it was not a good day, her consistent reply when specifically asked was, "I'm just not feeling as well today as I would like to feel." That was the end of the focus of the conversation on Mother.

Mother would always encourage me to travel when opportunities became available. She lived in our home, and this would mean having another caregiver in the home while we were away. It would have been very easy for her to tell me she wished I would not go and try to make me feel guilty for "leaving her." This never happened. She truly put others above herself.

Amelia

Starting Over

My sons, who were two and three at the time, and I moved to Georgia from Arizona with all our possessions. We moved into an apartment and I started a new job in Atlanta.

All was going well until, one day on my way home, I realized my apartment was on fire and was burning down. I called my job and told them I wouldn't be there the next day. I picked up my children from daycare and went back to see if there could be anything to salvage. As I stood there watching the fire and people crying, I turned to look at my children and they were playing with the buckets of favorite toys and blankets they took to the daycare that morning. Our home was gone and everything we owned. What do we do now?

Red Cross came and put us up in a motel for three days, gave us food and vouchers and clothes for those three days. Thanks to my employer I received another place to live, furniture, clothes, toys and food.

People do care.

Bernice

The Special Christmas Tree

My friend greeted me at the door. I handed her some flowers and turned to leave. She said that she wanted me to come in and see the "special Christmas tree" that she had decorated as one of her surprise gifts to her husband who was battling ALD (Lou Gehrig's disease).

As I was admiring the pretty tree, she told me why she had bought a white tree and decorated it with blue lights and blue ornaments. Over forty years ago, before their first Christmas together, she had gone to buy a tree and decorations. They were young and newly married, so there was not much money in the budget for this. All the green artificial trees were more expensive, but she found a white tree that was much cheaper and bought it. Also, she found some blue lights and blue ornaments that she could afford. Their first Christmas together was special and so was the white tree decorated in blue!

That tree, the lights and all but two of the original ornaments were discarded many years ago, but were not forgotten. My friend had a feeling that this might be their last Christmas together, so she went shopping and bought a white tree and blue lights and ornaments as similar to the originals as possible. She had the new tree completely decorated with the new lights and ornaments, along with the two original ones, when her husband saw it for the first time.

During the entire time of her husband's illness, both of them consistently exhibited a positive attitude during difficult times. The tree was one more example of my friend's positive attitude. In less than two months from Christmas, her husband was gone, but they enjoyed their last Christmas together with a "special tree."

Amelia

Wheelies

I was trying to teach my seven-year-old son about being kind to those who are different from him and also about being thankful for what we are able to do. I said, "Think about your friend in a wheelchair. It must be hard for him not to run and play, like the rest of the boys." My son's response was, "Maybe so, but he can really pop wheelies in his wheelchair! I can't do that!" Somehow my son had already learned to look for the positive in a situation that others maybe see as a negative.

Melodie

CHAPTER TWO

Laughter: Joy in the Middle of Junk
(Laughter and Humor)

"Trouble knocked on the door, but, hearing laughter, hurried away."
Benjamin Franklin

Do We Laugh Because We're Happy Or Are We Happy Because We Laugh?

News flash—Life can sometimes throw a bunch of junk at us! Charles Swindol, a popular Christian author and speaker, wrote a wonderful book called *Laugh Again*. In that book he wrote about refusing to let circumstances dominate our attitudes and using laughter to help us enjoy our lives in spite of what's happening.[1]

Too often I think we confuse the words joy, laughter and happiness. Happiness and joy are different. Outward circumstances for many people dictate whether or not they are happy. They say, "I would be happy if:

> Only I had more money.
> Only I had another job.
> Only I was prettier.
> Only I had a nicer house."

The following, called "A Beautiful Prayer," really helps us realize the difference between joy and happiness:

> *I asked God to take away my habit.*
> *God said, No.*
>
> *It is not for me to take away, but for you to give it up.*
> *I asked God to make my handicapped child whole.*
> *God said, No.*
>
> *His spirit is whole, his body is only temporary.*
> *I asked God to grant me patience.*
> *God said, No.*
>
> *Patience is a byproduct of tribulations:*
> *It isn't granted, it is learned.*
> *I asked God to give me happiness.*
> *God said, No.*
>
> *I give you blessings; Happiness is up to you.*
> *I asked God to spare my pain.*
> *God said, No.*
>
> *Suffering draws you apart from worldly cares*
> *and brings you closer to me.*
> *I asked God to make my spirit grow.*
> *God said, No.*
>
> *You must grow on your own, but I will*
> *prune you to make you fruitful.*

*I asked God for all things that I might enjoy life.
God said, No.*

*I will give you life, so that you may enjoy all things.
I asked God to help me LOVE others, as much as
He loves me.
God said...Ahhhh, finally you have the idea.²*

Source Unknown

At a dinner meeting I was speaking about the difference between happiness and joy, and a gentleman asked if I knew the definition of the word joy. Seeing my puzzled look, he said, "*JOY* stands for <u>J</u>esus, <u>O</u>thers, <u>Y</u>ou." You know, I think he was right. It is so easy to fall into the trap of thinking only about oneself—what *I* want or what will make *me* happy.

Instead we need to be thinking, *"What can we do to serve Jesus, others and then ourselves?"* It is also interesting that sometimes the best way to handle our own stress and find joy and smiles is to quit being so self-absorbed and do for others.

For example, a woman told me she was going through a very difficult time in her life—divorce, depression and other problems. She was becoming more and more self-absorbed, feeling very sorry for herself, and admitted that no joy or laughter was in her life. A friend suggested volunteer work, and she started working with underprivileged and abused children. The more involved she got with these children, the less she thought about her own problems. After some time she realized she was smiling again. What now brought her joy was hearing laughter from these children and seeing them open up and trust her.

Think about some people you know that are joyful, positive and enthusiastic about life. Rarely are they the ones with looks, titles or great possessions. Often they have experienced great challenges in life.

Clyde Taylor, my mother-in-law, was one of those rare people who could find joy in any situation. She did not have many material possessions and had little education, although she was one of the most intelligent and interesting people I have ever known. Her life was not easy, having raised seven children during hard times. Because of diabetes, she lost her sight and could no longer experience one of her favorite joys—reading. The diabetes progressed to the point that her leg had to be amputated, but I never heard her complain. In fact, what I remember her talking about was how blessed her life was. She smiled, laughed, and found joy in simple things. Each day was a gift to her. She loved God, she loved life, and it showed.

"Laughter is the sun that drives winter from the human face."

Victor Hugo

In the Bible we read about the apostle Paul, who was imprisoned and persecuted, yet his letters revealed a theme of joy and laughter. Paul refused to allow circumstances to steal his joy.

"I thank my God every time I remember you. In all my prayers for all of you, I always pray with joy..."

Philippians 1: 3-4

One Sunday my minister was talking about how a plant that is not pruned does not grow well, and that God often "prunes" us to make us grow as Christians. I was going through a *very* difficult time then and feeling sorry for myself. As I sat there and listened, I was thinking—*God, You must be pruning me to make me grow, but I feel that I've already been pruned back to the ground. What else is there?* Then I started smiling and laughing to myself and thinking—*All that's left are my roots, and I hope they are not next!* My husband leaned over and asked me what I was giggling about and I said, "My roots." You can imagine the expression on his face!

Laughter is truly a gift from God. He did not promise that life would be easy or that there would be no pain. He did promise that if we believed in Him, joy *could* come into our lives. It is our choice whether or not to look for it.

> "There is no oil without squeezing the olives,
> No wine without pressing the grapes
> No fragrance without crushing the flowers
> And no real Joy without sorrow."[3]
>
> Source Unknown

So many people have said to me, "When things get better, maybe my sense of humor will come back," or "How can I laugh when I have all these problems?" They cannot see past their immediate pain and hurt. I can understand their feelings. I worked with a breast cancer support group and not one of those women thought it was humorous when they were first diagnosed with breast cancer. However, most of them agreed that, as time went by, being able to find humor in their situations and being able to laugh helped them to cope.

> "Humor is tragedy plus time."
>
> Carol Burnett

Here is a comment from one cancer group member who used humor to cope with her situation.

A nephew called not long after my surgery for breast cancer. I was feeling quite mutilated at the time and dreading the thought of being a freak the rest of my life. He was asking about my progress and procedures, and I explained how I had been promised a reconstruction that would be better than the original. "That's funny," he said. "I stopped for gas today and two men were standing around the station talking. When I walked in, they asked me a question—'Can you tell the difference between a real breast and manufactured one?' I quickly replied that who cares, if she lets you close enough to decide for yourself?"

Sarah

Being able to look at life's situations with a sense of humor helps keep things in perspective. The following note I received is a good example:

Hello Merry,

Well, we were spared again! It is hard to believe that Hurricane Charley came so close to Hilton Head and I slept right through it. However, the sleep aid helped. There weren't any strong winds and no evidence of large amounts of rain. We will not always be this fortunate, and today we are grateful. Now we have to worry about friends north of us. Of course my son, John, was out surfing and I was in the bed with covers over my head. That method has protected me for years and it worked again!

Margie

"Against the assault of humor, nothing can stand."

Mark Twain

Humor can help break the tension of a stressful situation. Because my mother-in-law's leg was amputated due to complications from diabetes, she wore a prosthetic until her death a few years later. Several weeks after she died, my husband, five-year-old daughter and I were in her home cleaning, and walked into her bedroom. Propped up there against the wall was her artificial leg. My daughter took one look at it, mouth and eyes opened wide, and screams of terror came bellowing out as she fled the bedroom and house. Down the street she ran, screaming the entire way, and it took us several minutes to catch her. We calmed her down and finally laughed about it. Even today as a young woman my daughter talks about "Grandmother's leg."

After a workshop, I was talking with some of the participants about how humor is so important in helping get through tough times. One woman laughed and said humor was how she tolerated her mother-in-law. When asked what she meant, she told us her mother-in-law had hated her and made her life difficult, but that things were different now. She smiled and explained. Now that her mother-in-law had Alzheimer's disease, she had forgotten that she hated her and they got along fine!!

"Laughter is an instant vacation."

Milton Berle

Humor and laughter can help us cope. It does not make those stressful situations go away, but it sure can help us get *through* them. I have a very good friend who has MS, her husband has MS, her daughter has MS and her son is autistic. I wonder how many people have challenges like that? You might think she would be negative and resentful, with little joy or laughter in her life. Well, just the opposite is true. When we get together, the first thing we do is laugh.

We often joke about the saying that goes—*"Smooth seas do not make a skillful sailor"*—and vow that we ought to be great sailors, because we sure have had a lot of rough seas on which to practice. We might cry a little, but we laugh a lot, and she always has a smile for me when I'm down.

"If you can't make it better, you can laugh at it."

Irma Bombeck

When we talk about humor, we aren't talking about joke-telling, but about being able to laugh at life and ourselves. A joyful, but stressful, life event that many people can identify with is the blending of families. Humor and laughter certainly played a big role in helping our family with that transition.

When I remarried, there was a blending of four children, and that was a challenge for all involved. We were married in May and decided to have a *"family"* honeymoon in June to Disney World. The children were thirteen, eleven, nine and seven. The only vehicle we had that was large enough to accommodate the entire family was an old, banged up Toyota pickup truck. Trying to save money, we put the camper top on the truck, piled the kids in the back (while that was still legal) with blankets, pillows, food, drinks and games, and off we went to Disney World! Looking every bit like the Beverly Hillbillies, we headed down Interstate 95. The trip down there was not too stressful or eventful, since we were all excited and looking forward to having fun once we were there. Things went fairly well at Disney World, but like most families we started getting on each other's nerves by the end of the week.

The trip home was another story! It very quickly turned into arguments among the children with comments like, "You touched me," or "You ate my cookie," or "You breathed on me," and it went downhill from there. The back of the truck was actually swaying and rocking back and forth with all the pushing and shoving going on. It got so bad that several times my husband had to pull over in the emergency lane, drag a child out screaming and administer a spanking. Then off we went again on our long journey home. Through the years the story has probably been embellished a little (it really didn't need much)! At family dinners and gatherings we always laugh about our Beverly Hillbilly trip to Disney World and talk about how humor and laughter helped us handle the stress of trying to blend into a real family.

Humor also helps if you are a woman over fifty. Laughter has certainly helped me get through some stressful *clothing* challenges. One that comes to mind is the ordeal of trying on a bathing suit. There I am in the dressing room, tugging and pulling on a small piece of cloth that seems about the size of a postage stamp, trying to stretch it over an area the size of a shipping crate. If I could not laugh when I finally look into the mirror (especially from the rear view), I would either go into shock or cry!! Not only does laughter make us feel better, but studies indicate that it can improve our emotional and physical health.

> *"A joyful heart is good medicine, but a crushed spirit dries up the bones."*
> *Proverbs 17:22*

How Do We Find Laughter and Humor?

Most of us know people that make us feel better by just being around them. Probably one of the reasons is that they laugh a lot, and another is that they make *us* laugh. My husband is one of those people. When I am upset, stressed or "down in the dumps," he can always find a way to bring a smile to my face.

Many years ago there was one time when I came home from work very angry and frustrated. My husband tried everything to make me laugh, but I was determined to sit there and sulk and stew. About 15 minutes went by and I heard footsteps coming down the hall. Looking up I saw my husband casually stroll by wearing my son's cowboy hat, toy cowboy holster and guns around his waist, bandana around his neck, work boots, and *naked*! He did not say a word or look around, but just kept right on walking. I burst out laughing and almost fell off the sofa! My anger bubble just popped and disappeared. It is amazing what a good laugh can do for a person.

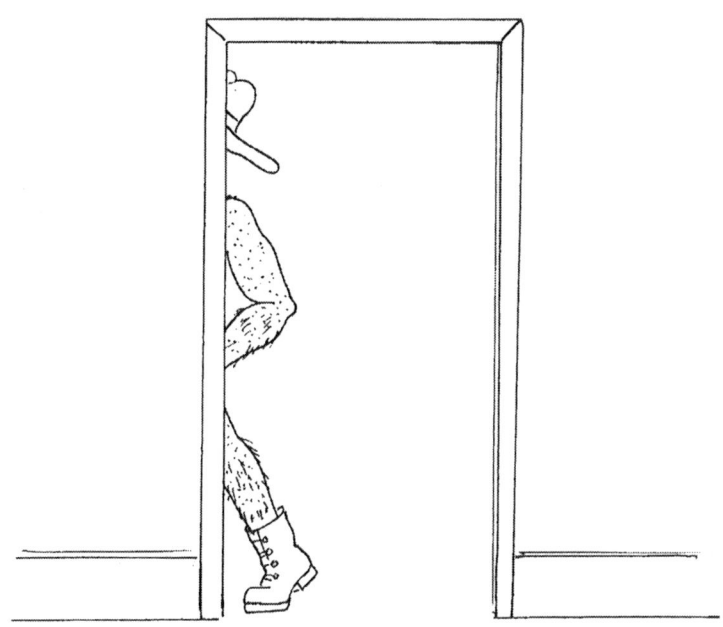

Surround yourself with positive people and those that make you laugh.

Even as a young girl growing up I realized the power of laughter. My mother had five sisters, and they grew up during the Depression with tough times. At family gatherings, unlike most other small children, my cousins and I would not go out and play. We would hide in a corner so we could overhear my aunts. There was always laughter... not just chuckles, but the knee-slapping, side-splitting kind. Most of the time we never knew what they were laughing about; we just "caught" their contagious giggles.

Read books that make you laugh. Watch movies that you think are funny or television programs that make you feel good. Someone once asked me if I watched the reality shows on television. After giving them the "look," I told them, "Absolutely not! My life is already too *real* to suit me." Viewing more stress or challenges of any kind was not what I wanted to do. Escaping a little from reality was my goal! Several years ago for Christmas my family gave me every volume ever taped of the Little Rascals. No matter how many times I watch them, they always make me laugh and feel better. Sometimes we just have to slow down our hectic and stressful lives long enough to look around and see things that bring us joy.

As I previously mentioned, our lives cannot be all "should's" and "have to's." There need to be some "want to's." Laughter and joy often come from these. There will always be stress and problems, but hobbies and outlets can help us temporarily escape from them. Through the years, however, I have been amazed at how many people do not have any hobbies or pleasant diversions. Playing with my grandchildren, walking my dog, riding my horses (or just hugging them), helping others, playing tennis, reading… all these things bring smiles to my face and joy to my heart. What fills your soul, brings you joy and puts a smile on your face? Think about it. What are your "want to's", and how often do you put them in your life?

"There is more to life than increasing its speed."

Ghandi

So many people have shared stories of how humor lightened their burdens and helped reduce stress. A man told me this story:

I had gone to a large midwest city to negotiate a multi-million dollar deal for my company. The meeting lasted all day and finally the negotiations totally broke down and everything that could go wrong did. Frustrated and angry, I went back to my hotel and sulked. Eventually, though still upset, I decided to go out and get a bite to eat. While waiting in line at the restaurant, I noticed a pretty little girl standing in front of me with her family. She was about four or five years old and had long blond hair with curls. To pass the time I decided to strike up a conversation, so I said, "Hi there." She said, "Hey." "You sure do have pretty hair," I said. She was shy and still had not looked up at me, but answered, "Thank you." (One thing I need to explain is that I am bald.) "Where did you get such pretty hair?" I asked. In a loud voice she answered, "Jesus."

"Jesus gave you your pretty hair?"
"Yes."

At this point she looked up at me, then at my baldhead, then back at my face, and said, "He took yours back, didn't He?" She was so serious, so literal, that I burst out laughing.

It was the only thing that day that made me smile, and it felt so good.

Does This Fig Leaf Make Me Look Fat?

A young man who worked at an insurance company shared this story:

I work in claims and am on the telephone about six hours a day, most of the time with irate customers, so it can be very stressful. One day had been terrible. I had been hollered at and cussed out all afternoon. About 4:00 pm the phone rang, and I answered it. An older gentleman said, "Do you cover Viagra?" I said, "Yes sir, we cover (pay) for eight a month." Since almost always the customer's next question is, "Why only eight?" I continued to explain the policy and didn't give the man a chance to say anything. He then interrupted me and said, "No, no, no. You don't understand. I don't want eight; I only want two. If my wife calls, don't you dare tell her you pay for more than two a month!" When we hung up, I started laughing and told my co-worker what had happened. We both sat there and howled. It felt so good to laugh after such a bad day.

Humor can also help put things back into perspective. A gentleman in Georgia told me he had a pond on his land. There was a large turtle eating small fish and being a nuisance, so he had tried several times to shoot it. One day he spotted it out in the water, got in his boat and rowed out toward the turtle. He picked up his rifle, looked into the sight and fired. To his surprise, he realized he had shot a hole in his boat!

Life is like that sometimes. We think we see things straight, clear and on track, but we really do not—and our actions can sink us!

"Laughter is the shortest distance between two people."

Victor Borge

Sometimes humor can help people with different personalities communicate and work together more effectively. Laughter can create a common bond. A woman who was Director of Medical Records at a large medical center shared this story:

I was at my desk one morning when the telephone rang. It was a doctor who had the reputation for being abrupt, demanding, stoic, and never smiling. He immediately lit into me and said, "Ms. Jones, what kind of shop are you people running up there? There has been a spelling mistake made in my patient's chart and it totally changes the meaning." My stomach knotted up, but I tried to keep my composure and answered, "Dr. Smith, I am not sure what the problem is, but I will be glad to look into it." He interrupted me and started laughing. "Ms. Jones, I am not really upset with you, but there has been a spelling mistake made and, believe me, it does change the meaning." He explained to me there had been a long study on this man's condition. What was supposed to be coded into the patient's chart was, "The study was remarkable." What got coded in by mistake was, "THE STUD WAS REMARKABLE!" We both started laughing and agreed it did change the meaning of the patient's chart, and ever since we have had a good working relationship.

"Humor is the great thing, the saving thing. The minute it crops up, all our irritations and resentments slip away and a saving spirit takes their place."
                                                                  Mark Twain

Humor and laughter often can be the only things that help us get through a stressful day at work. While presenting a workshop, I was chatting with a woman about how laughter can help break the tension of a demanding day or work environment. She told me this humorous story. She said the company was going through reorganization and times were very stressful. In her department there were some delays on critical information. Her vice-president sent out an e-mail announcing some technical problems and asked that everyone please *"BARE"* with him. Of course, it was supposed to be spelled BEAR. She commented that people had great fun with their responses, and the laughter helped everyone get through the stressful times.

Here's a story about how laughter broke the tension of a frustrating day for one nurse:

Things had gotten more and more hectic at the hospital. Our units were full; we were short-staffed and working double shifts. On this particular day, nothing had gone right, and I was tired, stressed and frustrated. It was almost the end of my shift, and I was on my way to the pharmacy, grumbling the entire time. I got off the elevator and started down the hall when I heard, "Help!" I stopped and looked around, but did not see anyone. In a few seconds I heard, "Help, help, let me out of here!" It was then I realized the sound was coming from the direction of the morgue. I walked to the morgue, knocked on the door and said, "Hello, is there anyone in there?" From the morgue came a voice screaming

Does This Fig Leaf Make Me Look Fat?

in a panic, "Help, help, let me out of here!" I tried the door, but it was locked, so I said, "Pull the door from the inside." The voice screamed, "It won't open; it won't open!" I thought for a second, and told him to use the phone in there and call security. A hysterical voice cried, "H#*# LADY, I AM SECURITY!"

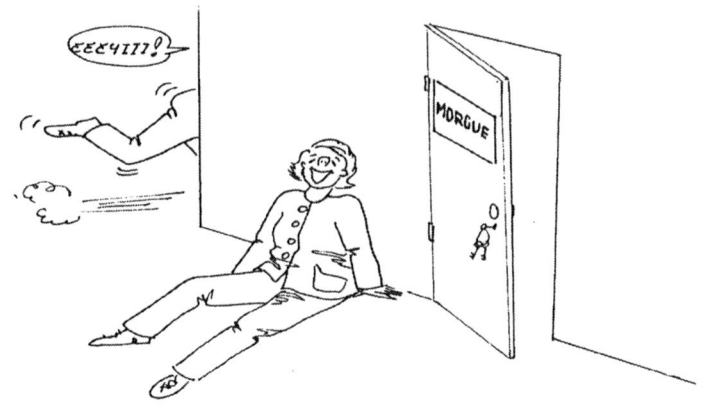

Suddenly it dawned on me that he should have keys. I suggested he try one of them, but he shouted that they did not work from the inside. I told him to slide the keys under the door, and I would unlock it from the outside. Then I got down on my hands and knees and waited. His hands must have been shaking violently because the keys were jumping all over. Finally, I grabbed them, put the key in the lock and heard a click. Instantly the door flew open, caught me square in the face and slammed me up against the wall. I never saw the man. All I heard were footsteps running down the hall and him screaming. Paralyzed with pain for a minute, I then peeled the door off my face and my body from against the wall. Once I realized my nose was not broken, I thought about how funny the situation was and started laughing. In fact, I was laughing so hard I slid down to the floor and just *sat there with tears running down my face. After a few minutes I got up, composed myself, and thought about how much better I felt after that GOOD LAUGH!*

"Always laugh when you can. It is cheap medicine."

Lord Byron

Sometimes we laugh to keep from crying and taking out our frustrations on other people. I had experienced a particularly bad week with a lot of negative, complaining people and was exhausted. It was a Thursday and I had my last workshop to teach that day and I just did not want to go. On that morning my husband left very early for a meeting. Later, I went out to my car, put the key in the ignition and heard that awful click we all have experienced. The battery was dead. What to do? I called my husband and he told me to drive the truck. Now let me explain. I drive a small, two-seat car. This truck was a Dually diesel, which seemed to me about two blocks long, and I had never driven it. After much struggle, I finally climbed (literally) into this thing and started off to work. To reach my training location I had to drive across a very long dam. Of course, a dump truck pulled right in front of me going about 15 miles per hour and I couldn't pass. I was thinking—*great, here I am teaching a time management workshop and going to be late. That will do a lot for my credibility!* Eventually I arrived at my location and went in to set up for the class. People started walking in and asking me the location of other classes on the campus. Trying to be accommodating, I stopped what I was doing and directed them to their classes. After about 15 people asked for directions, I headed back to my room. By this time it was after 9:00am, the starting time for my class. I really needed some coffee, so even though I was late, I stopped by the canteen to get some coffee out of a vending machine. It only took correct change, so I started rummaging through the bottom of my purse for coins. I finally found some, put the change in the machine, heard it start brewing, and then watched in horror as the coffee started pouring down—with no cup in place. I was so desperate for a cup of coffee that I actually considered leaning over and putting my mouth under the stream of coffee to get some caffeine. The only reason I didn't was because I was afraid my head would get stuck in the small area with the plastic sliding door, and then someone would see me or even have to pull my head out!

I could have become frustrated and angry, and taken it out on the participants in my class, but I had another choice—to laugh. And that's exactly what I did—just stood there and laughed. Then I walked back into the class and asked if they had ever heard of Murphy's Law. I shared my morning experiences and we all laughed and had a wonderful day together.

Laughter Lightens and Brightens Our Days

Because we are having a bad or stressful day, we frequently get tunnel vision and become stuck in the negative mode. There are many opportunities for humor and laughter. I am not talking about laughter at anyone else's expense, hurtful humor, making fun of others or putting people down. It's about using laughter to help rise above circumstances and lighten the day.

I was at a ladies' church luncheon and the women at our table were talking about how humor is so important in our lives. A woman told me that for years she taught the 3 and 4 year-olds in Sunday school. She said it could be exasperating and stressful, but that there was always a lot of laughter when dealing with children. She told me one Sunday a mother brought her 4- year-old son to class. When the boy walked in, the woman asked him where his father was, since he was usually with them. He said that his daddy had a terrible headache because he drank too much *tea* the night before!

Being able to laugh certainly helps chase away bad moods. A woman shared her story:

I was having a terrible day at work and was in a bad mood. During lunch I decided to run a few errands and zip through a burger joint for a bite to eat. The drive-thru line was not long, so I pulled in. The car in front of me looked like an old Plymouth from the 50's. Driving it was a little old lady who was so short her head barely reached above the steering wheel. I noticed the lady's head going up and down and side to side like she was looking for something. The lady sat and sat, without moving, and finally pulled her car up past the drive-thru window. She then started SHOUTING HER ORDER INTO A LARGE TRASH DUMPSTER.

Obviously this was her first visit to a drive-thru and she was just a little confused! I sat there and just chuckled. I was not making fun of her, but just enjoying how cute she looked. It is amazing what a good laugh can do for your attitude and mood. I went back to work in a totally different frame of mind.

Sometimes situations are not humorous at the time they happen, but later we can think back on them and laugh. A woman who was a manager of a Florida Credit Union told me her story that was initially embarrassing, but later she (and her staff) found great humor in it.

It had been an awful day at work. Nothing had gone right—angry customers, problems, employees snapping at each other... you name it. My office was on one side of the lobby and the ladies' room was on the other side. I had gone to the ladies' room and was walking across the lobby when I heard several female employees scream. One of them literally jumped across her desk, landed right behind me and said, "Keep walking." I said, "Get back, what in this world are you doing?" My employee was laughing so hard she could not answer and just kept pushing me towards my office. Finally, we arrived there and my employee slammed the door and said, "Look in the mirror on the back of your door." I turned around, looked, and almost fainted. My slip and dress were caught up in the top of my panty hose so my entire rear end was exposed. As if that were not bad enough, when I wear Control Top pantyhose I do not wear panties underneath my pantyhose. I had just walked across a crowded lobby with my BARE rear end showing!!

Does This Fig Leaf Make Me Look Fat?

Of course, at first I was mortified. As time passed, however, the "event" became a great stress buster. When the office would get stressful, one of the employees would start humming and say, "Moon over Miami." Then everyone would start laughing, EVEN ME!

Another woman told me how being able to laugh at herself certainly helped her through an embarrassing situation:

Several years ago, I received an invitation to a very dressy, fancy cocktail party. My husband refused to go but I wanted to go so much I decided to go alone. This was a black tie affair and the women would be in cocktail dresses and expensive jewelry. A friend loaned me a dress and a fake fox stole. This stole wrapped around the shoulder and had an imitation fox head on one end. When I arrived at the party, I walked into the room with the food and punch. The plates were small, but I picked up one and started loading it up with chicken wings, because I was very hungry. Next I headed toward the punch bowl and dipped me a cup of

Does This Fig Leaf Make Me Look Fat?

punch. It was difficult to balance all that, so I tried to get close to a wall to lean against it. With a plate in one hand and a chicken wing in the other, I was trying to balance my punch cup on top of my plate.

When I stepped back against the wall the heel of my shoe (very high heels) went into the grate. I put the chicken wing in my mouth to try and free up a hand. As I did, though, the stole swung off my shoulder and the fox head started flapping wildly in every direction.

When I tried to get my shoe out of the grate, the whole grate came off with my heel still stuck in it and I was tripping and dragging it across the room!! A policeman stationed at the far side of the room saw what was happening and came over to try and help. The problem was that he was laughing so hard he was doubled over and could not get any words out. People were gaping and staring, and I was mortified.

Finally the humor of it all hit me, and I also started laughing. When the policeman finally got my shoe out, people started clapping and laughing. They came over to tell me what a great sense of humor I had, and the tension just disappeared.

Laughter also helped reduce the stress of a complaining co-worker, according to the man in this story:

We had one employee in our office that complained all the time. He called in sick so much it was frustrating to everybody and we tried something to break the tension. When he called to say he was sick and would not be in, we would have a pool to see who could guess what his reason was this time. Each person would write down on a piece of paper the ailment and/or body part he thought was the problem. Then we put it in an envelope with a quarter and sealed it. When he got back to work and told what was wrong with him, we would open the envelopes and the person coming closest to his ailing body part would win the money!

Here is a humorous story from a dentist:

The day started off badly and went downhill from there. Late in the afternoon I went in to the examining room and there sat an older gentleman with an unusual expression on his face. My first thought was, "Who in the world fitted your dentures?" I greeted him and then tactfully commented that his teeth could probably be adjusted to fit a little more correctly. I then asked him where he got them fitted. He responded, "Nowhere. I bought them at a GARAGE SALE!" His answer shocked me so that I almost dropped my dental tools and had to turn my head to keep from showing my surprise. After he left I told the staff and assistants what the gentleman had said and we all had a good laugh.

Pulling Smiles from the Memory Banks

Some days we wake up and feel like this —GR-GR-GR-GR. We're thinking—*I hope somebody crosses me today; I just hope they do!* It's almost like we are looking for an excuse to be negative and then jump on somebody. I tell people as they go into work, smile, and when people ask how they are—lie! Don't start telling everyone about your ole rag husbands, kids or their operations. On those days it may be difficult to find anything to smile about. However, we all have had something really funny happen to us, even though it might have happened years ago. You know the humorous things I am talking about, the kind that double you over from laughing so hard. We never forget those because they feel so good. They are buried in our memory banks, so retrieve and focus on them during a particularly bad day.

One situation that happened to me about 20 years ago has helped me get through many a bad day by pulling smiles from my memory bank. If I live to be 90 years old I will never forget this little old lady. She will never know how many smiles she has brought to my face.

A local nursing home invited me to present a talk on stress management. I told them I would be delighted to come, but was not going to call it "Stress Management," because I would feel foolish trying to teach a group of 85-year-olds how to live longer by managing their stress. Since they have made it to that age, they're doing something right! I decided to call it, "Staying Motivated." The program was held in their social hall and I was standing at the front, waiting for them to come in. First came the ladies, dressed in their finest, and they walked in and sat down. Then came the older gentlemen, what few there were. My program was going to be only about 15 minutes long, because I had learned (from experience) not to talk any longer. They will tell you that you've talked long enough and to sit down!

Before I started, I looked around the room and tried to make eye contact with several of them, including a lady sitting right in front of me. I know I did a double take because she was looking up at me with a huge—and I mean huge—smile on her face. What I chose to believe was that she really must have been looking forward to this (ha). I talked about six minutes and made another sweep around the room for eye contact, and the lady was still looking up at me with a gigantic smile. Once again, what I chose to think was, "She likes me." When it was over, most of them came up to speak to me and then walked off. The little old lady with the big grin was still standing there. She then grabbed me by my sleeve, pulled me down toward her, and started shouting at me (she must have been hard of hearing). She said, "Do you know why I was smiling the whole time you were talking?" I said, "No, but I was hoping it was because you liked what I had to say." She said, "Naw, that's not it. I'VE GOT NEW DENTURES AND CAN'T CLOSE MY MOUTH." It was all I could do not to fall over laughing. She didn't give a rip about my talk. She just wanted me to know about her new dentures. I literally bit my lip trying to prevent myself from bursting out laughing. Giving her a hug, I rushed out to my car, leaned against it and laughed for a long time, thinking how good it felt to smile.

Does This Fig Leaf Make Me Look Fat?

More Humor and Laughter Stories

The Marker

To prepare for rectal surgery (in a hospital where I worked as a nurse) I wrote all over my body with black permanent magic marker, because I know about all the mistakes that are made in big hospitals (and to surprise the staff since I knew them).

On each breast—in big letters—NO
On abdomen—OTHER SIDE
On low back—MY NAME, WITH AN ARROW POINTING DOWN
No one ever mentioned it but I'm sure the Operating Staff got a big laugh.

Nancy

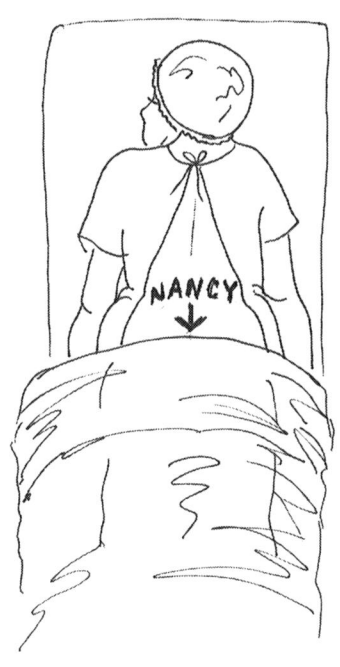

I've Heard It All Now!

One day at work, I received a frantic call from a patient. He stated, "My thing is broken." I said, "Sir, what thing?" He repeated, "My thing is broken." I said, "Sir, you can come to the hospital so we can determine what thing is broken."

The man came to the clinic and they sent him to Financial Counseling. I got this call from the supervisor stating, "You're to come down here and see this patient." When I arrived my staff was in tears and trying to suppress their surprise and laughter. I saw the man and said, "Sir, how can I help you?" He replied, "My thing is broken." It was then I noticed what he was talking about. His penile prosthesis was broken. He had one of those bendable ones and IT WOULDN'T GO DOWN. I took the patient to the clinic and told the patient he needed two thousand dollars to get the procedure done. He said, "I don't have two thousand dollars and my wife will leave me." I went to the administrator to get approval for the procedure. When I told my administrator what I needed two thousand dollars for, she burst out laughing. (I was twenty-five years old at the time.) She finally calmed down and gave approval. As a small hospital, we did not have these items on hand, so we had to order it. I told the patient and he told his wife.

Later that afternoon, I received a call from the patient's wife stating that if I did not fix his thing she was going to leave her husband. The whole process took three weeks. The patient's wife called here everyday for two weeks, still making the same threat. Finally a week later, the prosthesis came in and I called the patient. He retorted, "Aw, man! I don't need it now, she's left already!"

Stacy

Nap Time

On one of those hot South Carolina mornings, I was bass fishing one of my favorite lakes. I just happened to be fishing some docks when I noticed a banded water snake swimming in the shade of one of the docks I was fishing. I have no real fear of snakes so I didn't pay it much attention. As I made a cast under the dock I noticed this snake swimming toward me. I hit the trolling motor and moved on and he continued to follow. I sped up the trolling motor and he became discouraged and turned and went the other way. I motored to the next dock and continued fishing. In a few minutes I turned to pick up another rod and that snake was lying in the back of my boat enjoying the sunshine. I saw no real reason to panic, he was happy where he was, and I had another dock to fish. In a few minutes another fisherman I had met that morning came by and asked how I was doing, "You caught any yet?"

"No."

"Yea, me neither." "HOLY COW!" he yelled. "There is a snake in the back of your boat!" To which I calmly replied, "Shhh! I JUST GOT HIM TO SLEEP!"

Darrell

Hail, Hail

While living in Houston, Texas, one evening I was watching the movie, "Sword in the Stone," with my wife and 5-year-old son. At the end of the movie, a crowd of people was chanting, "Hail King Arthur, Hail King Arthur." My son turned to his mother and asked, "Mom, aren't they saying a bad word?"

I listened quietly as my wife explained that hail King Arthur was OK. It meant hurray for King Arthur. She further explained that hail from the sky was OK, but that hell where the devil lives was the bad word. Joshua seemed to accept the explanations and the subject was dropped.

Several weeks later I drove to South Carolina to look for new employment. I took my son along with me for company, since he would be able to stay with his grandparents. One morning Joshua and I left his grandparents to visit some friends. Joshua perched on the door arm of my blazer so that he would be able to place his elbow on the window edge as he rode, just like dad does. As we pulled onto the interstate highway, cars began zipping past us on both sides. My son looked around calmly and then said to me, "Dad, what the hail King Arthur is going on here?"

Steve

Fishy Tales

    I had set up a fish aquarium for my 3 ½-year-old son, Joshua. Late one afternoon my son was in his room and was very quiet. I was going to check on him as he met me in the hallway. He was holding out his hand to show me the fish he was carrying, which by this point was dead. I tried to explain to him that he cannot catch the fish or we would take down the aquarium. I explained to him that this is cruel and to wait until I get his daddy on the phone. So I did get dad on the phone, explained what had happened and that I wanted him to talk with Joshua. I put Joshua on the phone and his daddy proceeded to talk with him. Joshua's eyes got quite large and there was so much expression on his face and he said, "But daddy, that fish jumped right out of that tank and tried to bite me, so I caught it." I had to walk out of the room and laugh. Having been so upset in the beginning, I would not have imagined that I would have found humor in this.

Kathy

Admission Fee

When my daughter was 3 years old, we went to Sunday school every Sunday. We would give her older brothers money to put in the Sunday school offering. One Sunday morning I heard my daughter ask her older brother, who was 5, "Why don't I get any money?" He answered, "You're too young. You get in free. They don't charge admission for you."

Terry

D&C's—Oh Me!

Women have to develop a sense of humor to deal with all the "indignities" we put up with. For example, I wonder how many men would enjoy being spread-eagled on a metal table in the doctor's office and having the equivalent of a shoehorn inserted into them? My mother told me this story about one of her experiences with "female problems" and we have laughed about it for years.

Mother had recurring infections and female problems and had one D&C after another trying to correct them. One time she was in the holding area of the outpatient clinic, where the examining rooms are separated by cloth curtains that slide on rods. The nurse had positioned mother on the table, legs spread with feet in stirrups, sheet on upper part of body, but bottom area available and shining, waiting for the physician. The nurse walked out and tugged on the cloth curtain to close it, but something caught and the curtain did not close completely. The nurse was in a rush and didn't see what had happened. Mother said she was horrified because there she lay, spread-eagled for all the world to see. Before she could make a move to cover herself, she heard footsteps coming down the hall, so she just pulled the sheet over her head so no one would know who she was.

Does This Fig Leaf Make Me Look Fat?

As the steps passed a voice called out, "Hello, Mrs. Jordan, how are you today?" Mother said she recognized the voice as one of her GYN doctors and said at first she was mortified and embarrassed. Then the more she thought about it she just burst out laughing. She realized that she had been to that doctor so many times and had so many D&C's that he recognized her from THAT END just as easily as he did the other end (her face)!

Oh, the joys of being a woman.

Merry

The Subway

I accepted a professional position in Manhattan and my husband and I were hesitant to sell our house in South Carolina until we were more confident that my job would merit our relocation. Although I had traveled to New York City for business for years, I stayed in Manhattan hotels and was not accustomed to the daily commutes and habits of area residents. After my searching for a temporary residence, I settled on a one-bedroom, furnished apartment convenient to a subway to where I worked.

The following six months were about the most miserable of my adult life. I was alone and surrounded by nothing familiar to me, none of the comfort items my husband and I had accumulated, no family, friends or pets. Our upkeep in two separate places was far more expensive than we had planned. Also, problems with my being away while family members suffered illness, death, problems, etc., was both an emotional and physical drain, while trying to devote the professional time and energy required of me at that time.

One morning after my relocation, I awoke feeling particularly depressed about my situation. Knowing I couldn't allow myself to give in to feelings of desperation or regret, I dressed in an outfit that had always made me feel good about myself and put on a new lipstick in one of the newest bright colors. With my spirits lifted a bit, I held my chin in the air and trucked to the subway station two long blocks away for my commute.

Being about 5'2" tall, on a crowded subway with passengers holding onto ceiling straps, my head is at armpit level with most people. Trust me when I say this is a most unpleasant height to be while on a subway ride in a rush hour with no seats. I was too short to hang onto the straps, so I had to squeeze through other passengers and hope there was enough room to manage a hold on one of the vertical poles positioned throughout the subway cars.

Subway rides usually have jolting starts and stops, which cause humans standing upright to quickly sway back and forth, sometimes losing their balance, and teeter and slam into one another. Close quarters on hot subways with unsteady rides resulted in the most coifed and starched passengers emerging from subway tunnels appearing as if we had rooted for truffles in the wildest woods and smelling as if, well...I don't even want to go there.

This morning was a typical summer subway ride in rush hour. A big, well-dressed man standing in front of me was trying to read his neatly quarter-folded paper in one hand with his suit jacket slung over his arm, while holding the strap with the other. With every jolt, my head slammed into the side of his arm so, although wedged between people, he finally managed to turn his back to me to eliminate major reading interference.

My nose was then about 2 inches from his beautifully pressed white shirt back when the subway next slammed on brakes. To my horror, I planted a brightly colored, perfectly formed lip print right in the middle of his back. I was mortified! I didn't know whether to tell him or not and before I could decide, we came to his stop and he dashed from the subway car and was soon engulfed in the teeming crowd sweeping up the subway stairs.

Does This Fig Leaf Make Me Look Fat?

    At first I felt terrible, but the more I thought of it, the funnier it became to me. I pictured people's reaction, strangers and business contacts, as they encountered him all during the day. I imagined some of the questions he would have to field about this perfect, bright red lip print in the middle of his white shirt. I envisioned his own confusion about how in the world this lip print got on the back of his shirt and how, hopefully, that confusion turned into hilarity as the day passed. I found myself hoping his family had a good sense of humor and that he had a trusting spouse! I wondered if strangers went to work and told others, "I saw the funniest thing on the way to work," and if any fellow subway riders told their families over dinner about seeing a woman kiss the back of a shirt that morning.
    By the time I got to work, I was ready to tell everyone how I "kissed a shirt in the subway" and advised them all to let me know if they spotted it in the City that day. It gave a lot of co-workers a mission for the day and when someone left the mid-Manhattan building we worked in, they would call on their return and report that they didn't see the 'shirt' on the street while they were out.

I've recalled many times through the years how my kissing the white shirt ended up brightening up a day on which I was lonely and depressed, and how others had fun with it as well. The incident still brings a smile to my face as, by the end of the day, I felt as if I had received a bright red kiss with a perfect lip print from life for my very own self!

Rosemary

The Gift of Laughter

Laughter is truly a gift from God. I don't know how anyone survives without it. I grew up in a fairly large family and my dad used to say, "If you think God doesn't have a sense of humor, just tell Him YOUR plans!" That pretty much tells you where I come from.

When my father was diagnosed with prostate cancer, he went to our young minister for counseling. This young minister was very serious minded and didn't always look on the lighter side. Daddy said he had to stop going because he was getting depressed listening to the minister's problems!

Life has so many serious, mind-boggling situations. If all we focus on is the serious, I think we miss out on a very important part of the journey.

Ann

One Last Laugh

My father always kept "super glue" on hand because he was able to use it to fix most anything. After my dad died, my family was gathered at the funeral home awaiting his "Rosary" and visitation service. He was "lying in state" (so to speak) in the gathering room while we were waiting for the service to begin. I was standing at his coffin, and reached down to touch his face and noticed that one of his eyes had opened. I told my immediate family (mother, children, husband, siblings and nieces) what had happened as I went to get the woman that worked at the funeral home. "Ms. Evelyn" said not to worry, that she would take care of the situation. She came back to the room with a small "fix it" box and out she pulls a TUBE of SUPER GLUE!! She used it to glue his eyelid back in place!

This was my Dad's "One Last Laugh." I thank him for giving my family and me the ability to laugh in order to help get through difficult situations.

Martha

The US Mail

April 29th, 2004, forever changed my life. My husband, son and I had to fly from South Carolina to Texas for an emergency. My parents had an automobile accident (while on vacation) in which my dad died and mom was hospitalized. On the way there my son became very ill. Once there, many decisions had to be made and this was very difficult, being in a strange town, with my mom in pain and my father just having died. We had to decide how to get my mom back to SC and what to do about my dad. It was the most stressful time and the loss was painful.

Once we were on the plane back home, I started to laugh and my husband asked what was so funny. One of our decisions was that my dad was cremated and his remains were sent back to South Carolina to my pastor. I told my husband, "Dad used to get so upset with the mail. What if the post office loses dad?" My husband looked at me and we exploded with laughter! Dad would have laughed over this too. I smiled—dad had given me his sense of humor.

Melodie

Able to Laugh Again

While I was in the beginning of a very difficult divorce, I took my daughter, who was 8 years old at the time, with me to look at an apartment for us. I held it together while hearing information from the apartment agent, and even while going to look at the different apartments. However, when I went back to the apartment office to complete paperwork, I began to cry, turning away from my daughter to prevent her from seeing me break down. Well, she noticed and came around the table to see me crying. She laid her hands on my shoulders and said, "Mama, why are you crying? Is it because you don't have a husband anymore?" This made me cry a little harder and then she said, "It's okay, mama, you still have me and our kitty, Midnight!" I gave her a big hug, realized she was right, wiped away the tears and even had a smile on my face. I realized through the innocence of a child that we were going to be all right.

I have continued to use the strength she gave me on that day to assist me in the journey I am still on through the divorce process. She has helped to keep me focused and also enabled me to laugh again. We take the time now to create memories and enjoy life around us.

Nora

The Dangerous Sandwich

I worked in an in-patient Alzheimer's Unit at a large medical center and found it very rewarding, but also sometimes very draining. Very quickly I learned that a good sense of humor and being able to laugh at oneself was vital.

One story sticks out most, where I really needed to be able to laugh to help me deal with the stress. I had bought a sub sandwich for my lunch and placed it on the communal table located in the center of the unit. One of the patients, a little ol' lady who loved to hoard things, eyed my sandwich. I noticed her heading for it, so I ran to grab it before she did. She beat me to it and, in her state of mind, viewed me as an attacker. She whirled the plastic bag that the sandwich was in above her head and used my lunch to beat me. Lettuce was flying everywhere as I ran out of the room and down the hall with her on my heels.

Needless to say I went hungry that day. However, I just laughed and decided at least I got some exercise.

Jennifer

CHAPTER THREE

Feeling Like a Raggedy Ann In a Barbie World

(Self-Esteem, Purpose)

"Low self-esteem is like driving through life with your hand-brake on."
Maxwell Maltz

This Thing Called Self-Esteem

Have you ever felt like all the other women in the world have it together except for you, or that they are prettier, smarter, thinner, richer, funnier, more talented, wittier, or younger? If you have (and you know you have), then join the crowd!

What we're talking about is this thing called self-esteem or self-worth. Basically, self-esteem is how we feel about ourselves. It's so very easy to allow outside situations, events and people to mold us or rob us of our self-esteem. This is hurtful enough in itself, but I think there is a direct relationship between self-esteem and stress. It's not that people with good self-esteem don't experience stress; but if we believe in ourselves and our self-esteem is based on Christian foundations, we have more ability to manage the stress. Plus, since stress is our perception of what's happening to us, people with low self-esteem often *create* their own stress.

From my experiences I have found that women seem to be especially vulnerable to, and influenced by, society. Perhaps it's because women tend to assume the roles of buffers, pacifiers, and pleasers, and because society places more emphasis on outward appearance for women.

Where Do We Get Our Self-Esteem?

Most women have never really thought about all the things that influence self-esteem or how we feel about ourselves. One powerful influence comes from our parents and our childhoods. My mother and father always told me how smart and pretty I was; so I believed them. Several years ago I was looking through some old family pictures and I came across some photographs of myself at about 12 or 13 years old. A beauty I was not—pudgy, freckles and frizzy hair! But, I certainly *felt* valued and pretty, because my parents made me feel that way.

The problem is that for some people, their parents planted and nurtured seeds of self-doubt and poor self-worth. This was the case for Glenda, a woman in a weight management class I was instructing. Glenda had very poor self-esteem and I was puzzled as to why she was so "down" on herself. I asked her about her marriage, job, friends, and family. When I mentioned her father, her voice quivered, and tears came into her eyes. "My father was an alcoholic," she said, "and when he was drinking he was very verbally abusive." She looked right into my eyes and said, "Do you know that I can never remember him ever saying anything nice to me? It was always stuff like, 'You're so fat and ugly. No man will ever want you and I'll be stuck with you.'" She told me that he repeated that to her over and over during her childhood. She started to play that same tape in her own head, and eventually came to believe it.

Another example of how events in childhood can have long-lasting effects on our self-esteem came to light during a stress management coaching session. Henry was referred, initially, because of stress-related health problems. He worked as a researcher and writer in a small organization. Henry held a PhD and was one of the most intelligent people I'd ever met. He did his job so well that he was promoted to manager, which involved supervising several people. Henry didn't want this position, but was afraid to turn it down. After working in the new position for several months—and hating it—stomach and intestinal problems (including diarrhea) started. The symptoms grew progressively worse. Henry finally went to a doctor who prescribed medication, but also suggested using breathing techniques when he felt his stomach start to knot up. However, he didn't *show* Henry how to do them.

Henry and his wife were invited for dinner at the company owner's home, but dreaded going because he was a shy, introverted person. After their arrival and a few minutes of "small talk," Henry ran out of things to say and started feeling self-conscious. His stomach began knotting up and he was afraid of having an attack of diarrhea. Henry then remembered what the doctor told him, so he started taking quick breaths. A few seconds later Henry hyperventilated and passed out *face first into his dinner!*

This is when Henry started stress management coaching sessions. He told me that was the most humiliating experience of his whole life and that he would do anything to change and become more assertive and confident.

Henry, even though he had a doctorate, was wracked with self-doubt. Just like Glenda, he had a very abusive, critical father. Henry told me that no matter what he did, it was never good enough for his father. If he brought home five A's and one B, his father would call him stupid and berate him. Consequently, he grew up feeling like what he did was never good enough.

I worked with Henry for about eight months. One day he came into my office and laid a piece of paper on my desk. It was an invitation for him to present one of his research papers at a regional conference. Now keep in mind this was a man who passed out because he was so nervous and insecure just going to dinner at his boss's house. I asked him what he was going to do and he said he didn't know. Then I asked him what he *wanted* to do. To my surprise, he said he wanted to do it, but was scared. We began working on ways to reduce his fears and he presented his research paper at the conference. When he returned home, he called me and told me about his accomplishment. That's when I told him he had "graduated" from our sessions. I didn't hear from him for about two years. Then one day I received one of his research newsletters and was puzzled as to why he sent it. I looked it over and when I came to the back page, scribbled in the corner was this note—"*to Merry Taylor for helping me enjoy life again.*" I still have that newsletter.

School experiences also affect the development of self-esteem. Too often I have seen people who struggled in school and were quickly labeled as below average. Each year the story would repeat itself ... below average, low section, low achiever ... slowly but surely the molding of a poor sense of self-worth.

Probably one of the strongest and most negative influences on self-esteem, especially for young women, is the pervasive emphasis on looks in our society today. Let's face it, how many girls and women look like Barbie? Give me a break. Or how many look like the women in *Playboy* or the *Sports Illustrated* Swimsuit Issue? Those bathing suits they wear wouldn't fit my right arm! I love this quote from Barbara Johnson, author of many books on humor and self-worth, *"I'm really a perfect size 10, I just keep it covered in fat so it won't get scratched."*[1]

The media, movies, television and magazines bombard us with pictures of what they think beauty is. Here are some statistics, according to the information on the internet, which we "normal" women might find interesting:

- Marilyn Monroe wore a size 14.
- If Barbie were a real woman she'd have to walk on all fours due to her proportions.
- The average woman weighs 162.9 pounds (National Center for Health Statistics).
- One out of every four college-aged women has an eating disorder.
- A psychological study in 1995 found that three minutes spent looking at a fashion magazine caused 70% of women to feel depressed, guilty and anxious.

It's no wonder anorexia, bulimia, and other eating disorders are rampant among young women. It's not uncommon now for young women in their teens or early twenties to have plastic surgery so they'll fit society's standard of beauty. What they're doing is basing their self-worth and value on external appearance and external influences.

Maxwell Maltz, MD, F.I.C.S., a famous plastic surgeon, discovered something powerful about self-image. He found that many people who wanted surgery didn't really need it, and began to realize that their real problem was not their physical appearance. Instead, it was their inner, hidden self-image. They blamed how they felt on how they looked, and hoped plastic surgery would change everything. But Dr. Maltz discovered that even if he did the surgery and changed their outward looks, these people remained as unhappy as ever.[2] There's nothing wrong with helping nature along (might do it myself one day), but we need to do it to *enhance* our self-image, not to *define* it.

Sometimes, however, there is apparently no rhyme or reason for a person's self-esteem issues. I've known people with very low self-esteem who had loving, encouraging parents, positive school experiences, and were very physically attractive. So, what's another factor in influencing self-esteem? Genetics. People are "wired" a certain way. We inherit certain traits. For example, a person has three children and their personalities might be as different as night and day. We're born with different traits, and then life experiences influence us and mold us.

Usually we think of a person with a poor self-esteem as an underachiever. However, that same low self-worth can drive the person to become an overachiever or a perfectionist who is never satisfied with anything she does. Low self-worth can be destructive emotionally and physically. Some people are so self-absorbed that they can never focus on anything but themselves...their looks, weight, clothes, house, and material possessions.

> *"We make a living by what we get, but we make a life by what we give."*
>
> Sir Winston Churchill

"Self-respect cannot be hunted. It cannot be purchased. It is never for sale. It cannot be fabricated out of public relations. It comes to us when we are alone, in quiet moments, in quiet places, when we suddenly realize that, knowing the good, we have done it; knowing the beautiful, we have served it; knowing the truth, we have spoken it."

Noel Coward

When people constantly put themselves down or put others down, poor self-esteem or self-worth is probably a factor. A likely reason for this is that they are looking to the wrong sources for guidance. The best source for developing a healthy, Christian self-worth is the Bible. When we look to the Bible and God to help us with our problems, including self-esteem, we are better able to put everything into the proper perspective. Then, with His help, we find the strength and guidance to make better decisions. Consider the following Bible verses:

"...Do not think of yourself more highly than you ought, but rather think of yourself with sober judgment, in accordance with the measure of faith God has given you."
Romans 12:3

"You made him a little lower than the heavenly beings and crowned him with glory and honor."
Psalm 8:5

Improving Self-Esteem

So, what can women do to have a healthy self-esteem? First we turn to God and use His strength to give us guidance and direction.

Then think PMS. No, not the PMS you've probably got in mind. This PMS represents:

Physical *Food/Weight, Aging, Body Image*
Mental/Emotional *Stress, Attitude, Motherhood, Family, Friends, Relationships, Emotions*
Spiritual *Gifts, Dreams, Talents, Goals, Christian Walk*

These are some of the areas that women need to focus on during their journeys for positive self-worth.

Physical

Weight and Body Image

We've already mentioned many issues involved in this area. It's amazing how, as we get older, we develop more empathy. For example, I wore a size six until I was in my mid-forties. During those slimmer years I was working with a local hospital as a consultant with their weight-loss programs. When I would see overweight women talking about having difficulties either losing or maintaining weight, I would think—*just try harder*. I also remember women saying to me, "It must be my thyroid," and I would think, *yeah, right*.

Several years ago, when the weight started to "jump" on me, those words and thoughts came back to haunt me. I visited my family doctor and said, "I can't seem to lose weight; it must be my thyroid!" He laughed and said, "Merry, I'll run the test, but it's not your thyroid, it's your AGE." (The truth hurts.)

Now that I'm just a little (ha) past forty, something my mother told me really hits home. She said, "Merry, the older you get, you have to work twice as hard to just break even."

Part of having a healthy self-esteem is to be the best you can be for your age and situation. Sometimes, though, that's easier said than done. For example, all the women on my tennis team are younger and wear either a size two or four. The really frustrating part is that they *eat*. On our out-of-town tennis trips they pack it in. One team member said she read that being happy burns up more calories. Guess I'm just not as happy as they are!

People struggle with body image, weight and health issues at every stage of life. I'm a baby boomer. In fact, I was born in 1946 and Linda in 1947, the first generation of the baby boom. We boomers are facing many changes now in the physical aspects of our lives. The challenge is to be the best we can be for our age. We shouldn't just focus on sheer vanity as it relates to weight and body image, but also on well-being, energy and balance.

If people rely on Madison Avenue as a benchmark for physical areas such as body image, weight, aging, etc., it will be difficult to keep a healthy self-image. The way to grow a healthy self-esteem begins with God's standards.

"...The Lord does not look at the things man looks at. Man looks at the outward appearance, but the Lord looks at the heart."

1 Samuel 16:7

Remember, a healthy self-esteem starts from the inside out, not the outside in. So what are some ways to develop a positive self-esteem? You can pray, care for others, care for yourself, laugh, volunteer, exercise and squeeze joy out of life. Focus on what you do have, not on what you don't have. These will give you a good head start on improving your self-esteem.

Aging

"By the time you're eighty years old you've learned everything. You only have to remember it."

George Burns

"Sure I'm for helping the elderly. I'm going to be old myself someday."

Lillian Carter (at age 85)

This aging thing puzzles me. Everyone wants to live a long life, but no one wants to get old. Figure that one out. Once again American society makes it tough on us as we age. We are a youth-oriented culture and nobody wants to tell their ages because they are embarrassed. Not me. I'm just proud to be alive and kicking for another year. I love what comedian Phyllis Diller once said when asked her age, *"Well, biologically, I'm 70 years old, but because of plastic surgery no two parts of my body are the same age!"*

Some interesting things do happen, though, as women get older...

- We walk down the street and catch a glimpse of our reflection in a store window and wonder *who* that old woman is.
- We see a picture in the paper of a woman who died and think, *boy, she is really old*—and find out she is our same age or *younger.*
- We go to a high school reunion and think everyone looks so old and say to ourselves, *"I'm glad I don't look like that!"*
- Our GYN doctor looks like he or she is about 12 years old.
- Young people start putting the word "Miss" in front of our first name when they talk to us.
- We start looking at women our age and older to see what hair color they have.

Rodney Dangerfield had a funny quote about aging. He said, *"I'm at the age now where food has taken the place of sex in my life. In fact, just last week I had a mirror installed over my kitchen table."* You know, maybe that's why I've heard of a chocolate cake called "Better than Sex Cake."

I love the story told by Dr. Alexander Leaf in the *National Geographic* article about long-lived people:

Miguel Carpio, 123 years of age and the oldest citizen of Vilcabamba, continues his fondness for the opposite sex. According to his daughter he still likes to flirt with the girls, and was quite a ladies' man in his younger day. Says he: "I can't see them too well anymore, but by feeling, I can tell if they are women or not." Miguel has been heard to remark, "Oh, to be 108 again!" [3]

Something that really made me think about how young people view aging happened in a customer service class I was instructing. A young man, about twenty-eight years old, was talking about an irate customer who walked into the office. He said to me, "This woman was very angry and she was old, I mean *really old*. She looked like she was at *least* fifty-one or fifty-two years old." After I regained my composure, I said, "Boy, she *is* old. I don't see how she was even walking!"

After being bombarded with all these self-esteem-stealing issues, I just go back to the Bible. Joshua 13:1 tells us about all the plans the Lord had for Joshua.

"When Joshua was very old and well advanced in years, the Lord said to him, 'You are very old, and there are still very large areas of land to be taken over.'"

Believers never retire from God's service. We just assume another role and serve God, and what better way to feel valued and beautiful.

A woman that has been an inspiration to me is Faye. When I met her she had just turned 100 years old. You would never know that, however. I interviewed Faye for a program on attitude and found her to be an amazing woman. She drove until she turned ninety-nine and voluntarily gave up her driver's license. She belonged to a book club and a Bible study group, because she didn't want her mind to get stale! Faye also mentored medical students to help them understand the needs of older patients.

When I met her, *I* felt dowdy—you should have seen her clothes and hair. She took no medicines and had a better memory than I do. She was a Christian and an inspiration never to give up and stop trying.

> *"The hardest years in life are those between ten and seventy."*
>
> *Helen Hayes (at 73)*

Somewhere I came across the following poem. It certainly promotes the right mindset about aging, health and life:

"I'm Fine"
There is nothing whatever the matter with me
I am just as healthy as I can be,
I have arthritis in both my knees
And when I talk, I talk with a wheeze.
My pulse is weak, and my blood is thin,
But I'm awfully well for the shape I'm in.

My teeth eventually have to come out
And my diet—I hate to think about;
I am over weight and I can't get thin,
But I'm awfully well for the shape I'm in.

I think my liver is out of whack
And a terrible pain is in my back,
My hearing is poor, my sight is dim;
Most everything seems to be out of trim,
But I'm awfully well for the shape I'm in.

I have arch supports for both of my feet,
Or I wouldn't be able to go on the street,
And in the morning I'm just a sight,
My memory's failing, my head's in a spin,

> *I'm practically living on aspirin,*
> *But I'm awfully well for the shape I'm in.*
>
> *The moral is, as this tale we unfold,*
> *That for you and me who are growing old,*
> *It's better to say "I'm fine" with a grin*
> *Than to let them know the shape we're in.* [4]
>
> Author Unknown

One of my very favorite quotes is the following:

> "Some people, no matter how old they get, never lose their beauty—they merely move it from their faces into their hearts."
>
> Source Unknown

Mental/Emotional

Attitude

To improve our self-esteem in the emotional and mental areas, the important first step is to look at our attitude as it compares to God's plan for us.

On the following checklist, adapted from I Corinthians 13, place a mark where you think your attitude generally falls in relation to each comparison.

God's Love Plan	Our Human Nature
Patient	Impatient
Kind	Unkind
Content with what I have	Envious
Doesn't boast	Boastful
Humble	Proud
Not rude	Rude
Unselfish	Selfish

Slow to anger . . . . Quick to anger
Doesn't keep score . . . . Scorekeeper
Rejoices in truth . . . . Delights in evil
Protects . . . . Harms
Trusts. . . . . Doubts
Hopes . . . . Lacks hope
Perseveres . . . . Gives up
Never fails. . . . . Fails

After you look at where you put yourself in each comparison, think about *why* you chose that point. Does your attitude tend to fall more in the positive or negative mindset? If you'd like to see yourself as others see you, ask a family member, a friend, and a co-worker you trust to rate your attitude based on these same criteria. Be forewarned, you may by shocked by their answers!

One of the most powerful influences on our self-esteem is something we've already mentioned—self-talks. When we constantly play negative self-talks in our heads, we erode our feelings of self-worth. This serves to reinforce the idea—*if we say something to ourselves long enough, we will eventually believe it.*

Look at the following negative self-talks. Put an x beside the ones you feel you play in your head too often.

_____ 1. No one cares about me.
_____ 2. I can't do anything right.
_____ 3. I'm not smart enough for that.
_____ 4. I'm in this all by myself.
_____ 5. Nobody listens to me.
_____ 6. I might as well be invisible.
_____ 7. I have made too many mistakes.
_____ 8. I'm ugly.
_____ 9. I don't fit in with them.
_____10. I'm not very lovable.

_____11. I feel so guilty.
_____12. I'm worried.
_____13. I'm scared.
_____14. I cave in too easily.
_____15. God doesn't hear me or He'd do something.
_____16. I can't shake this bad habit.
_____17. It's hopeless.
_____18. I may as well quit trying…it's no use.
_____19. I'm so fat (skinny, or out of shape)
_____20. It seems like I take one step forward and two steps backward.

The Bible addresses every one of these issues. Read each of the following Bible verses. Then rewrite the negative self-talks you checked above, using these verses as a guide:

- Psalm 4:8
- Psalm 55:22
- Proverbs 3:26
- John 8:32
- John 15:9
- John 15:11
- John 15:15
- John 15:16
- Acts 1:8
- Romans 8:1
- Romans 8:16
- Romans 8:20-25
- Romans 8:31-34
- Romans 8:37
- Romans 8:38-39
- 2 Corinthians 12:7-10
- Ephesians 1:7-8
- Ephesians 2:17-18
- 1 Peter 2:9

A woman in one of my workshops shared with me that she was raped when she was seventeen years old. It was a terrible emotional experience for her and everyone told her not to go to trial, because it would just make things more degrading. She told me that at first she agreed with them. She then decided to press charges, because this man had been accused before and none of the other women would follow through. The opposing lawyer treated her as if the rape were her fault and her self-esteem plummeted. With God's help, counseling, and family support she pulled herself up, held her head high, and decided to volunteer with a rape support network. This way she helped other young women whose lives and self-esteem had been torn apart.

To improve our self-esteem we need to take an honest look at our lives, pray to God for help, keep a sense of humor and the right mindset. In *How to Relax in a Busy World,* Eve and Floyd Corbin write, "If you have been in the habit of inviting negative thoughts—jealousy, envy, resentment, and self-pity, think of these as intruders in your mind. The old Chinese saying fits here: 'You cannot stop the birds of the air from flying over your head, but you need not let them nest in your hair.'"[5]

Belinda was a weight management client. I suggested she keep a journal and one day she asked me to read one of her journal entries. It was so rewarding to see how her self-image was growing as she changed her perspective on things.

This is what she wrote:

Something humorous and wonderful happened today. I want to save it. I had bought a chocolate bar from Tabitha and was eating it on the way home. About half way through it I became bothered, realizing that I was out of control.

I asked the Lord to help me, reminding myself that I had not and would not be successful at eating healthy without His help. I had one more section. I guess, believing that God would probably disdain me for my weakness, I planned to finish it.

The last section fell off my lap to the floorboard. When I looked down I saw that it was not within my reach. As soft as it was, I knew that if I retrieved it, sand and dirt would be stuck to it.

Then I remembered that I had just asked the Lord for help. I asked Him for help and He helped me. The humor of it hit me. I laughed aloud and I wondered if the Lord was laughing too, with me. Christ and I laughed together. The thought still makes me smile. I feel very sure that God has a sense of humor. I pray that I get to enjoy it again soon. I'll look for it.

Belinda

You've heard the expression "being your own worst enemy." When dealing with stress and life, that's often the case. There are real problems out there—deaths, divorces, illnesses, traffic, layoffs. But some people make things worse because of their own personality traits and characteristics.

"The bow too tensely strung is easily broken."
Publius Syrus (1ˢᵗ century BC)

For example, there are some women I would call normal worriers. Everybody worries occasionally. However, some could be hired as *"professional"* worriers, because they have had so much practice and do it so very well! One of the first places to start in managing stress is to take a close look at our own personalities and decide which of our personality traits help us and which traits hurt us.

PERSONALITY ASSESSMENT

Rate yourself (honestly) using the following scale:

1-almost never 2-seldom 3-frequently 4-almost always

__I try to control.
__I make mountains out of molehills.
__I finish other people's sentences.
__I worry.
__I've been told that I need to relax.
__I need to be doing something all the time.
__I'm frustrated when others don't know what I want and when I want it.
__I've been called a perfectionist.
__I have a sense of time urgency.
__I find myself thinking or feeling aggravated, irritated or frustrated.
__I don't delegate because I'd just have to do it over again.
__I take things personally.

Range:
00-25   Your personality traits work for you
26-37   Moderate
38-48   Your personality traits make you more vulnerable to stress

An interesting thing happened at the end of a program where the participants had answered the personality assessment. A woman stood up (the manager) and apologized to her staff. She told the group she hadn't realized what a demanding and impatient personality she had. She then told us this humorous anecdote. It happened during a routine visit to her gynecologist. After her examination she went into the doctor's office and told him she thought she needed some medicine. The doctor asked her, "Are you depressed?" "No." "Are you tense?" "No." "Are you confused?" "No." "Then what kind of medicine do you need?" "A pill for irritation and impatience." The doctor smiled and said they didn't have a pill for that. The woman then said, "Well, that #**# me off!!"

Linda Sloan shares the following humorous story, which also illustrates how impatience and a sense of time urgency can affect our stress level.

You have probably been in a church service during which some brave pastor or lay person calls the young children forward to deliver a mini-sermon aimed at their level of understanding. I have been in this perilous position many times! Think about how you might have reacted in the following situation:

The children are gathered about you, squirming and poking and giggling among themselves. You begin to speak: "Good morning! Today I'd like..." That's as far as you get before four-year-old Becca raises her hand and starts calling your name. You glance her way and ask her to wait just a minute. The hand goes down and you proceed. "Today I'd..." The hand is back in the air and now she's standing, calling your name and moving toward you. Knowing when you've lost, you say, "Yes, Becca, what is it?" She begins, "Um...I...want to tell you about what happened..." (she pauses, turns around, scans the crowd, finds a familiar face and waves frantically)... "I want to tell you about what happened the other day at my house...no...it wasn't at my house, um..."(she reaches down, scratches a mosquito bite, giggles and proceeds...). "um...it was last week...and my aunt, she, um..."(she sighs)"...no that's not right.. I want to tell you um...what happened the other day at my house."

If, while just reading this scenario, you find that you're screaming to yourself, "SPIT IT OUT KID! WAS IT YOUR

AUNT OR YOUR UNCLE? WAS IT THIS WEEK OR LAST WEEK? WE NEED TO MOVE ON!" ...then you now have a true understanding of the effect the impatient and time urgent personality can have on our insides. Believe it or not, there are people in this world who could calmly and patiently sit there and wait for Becca to finish her story in her own good time!

Family and Motherhood

> "When my kids become wild and unruly,
> I use a safe playpen.
> When they're finished, I climb out."
> Erma Bombeck

I think women tend to feel more day-to-day stress because of our emotional ties as wives, mothers, caretakers, employees and friends. For some reason, women feel it's our job to make sure everyone is happy. And when someone is not happy (which, of course, is a great deal of the time), women take on the pain and stress. So ironically, those very traits or qualities that make women good nurturers also lead us to feel more stress; therefore, they get in the way of our caring for our own needs.

Oh, Motherhood! It can be the best and worst thing for our self-esteem. A new baby in our arms and we feel so fulfilled and complete; a new baby crying all night and we feel so helpless and inadequate.

We adopted Allison when she was three days old. Because of breathing problems she was put on an apnea monitor, and the alarm on it went off several times a night, waking everyone. Even when the monitor didn't alarm, Allison just didn't sleep.

When she was about eight months old, one morning around 3:00 am she was wide awake and crying out. I was at my wit's end and ready to try anything to get her to sleep. Finally, I remembered something my grandmother told me about giving babies a touch of brandy to help them sleep. Well, there was no brandy in the house, but I remembered some Kahlua being in the cabinet. Desperate, I took Allison's bottle, screwed off the top, poured in some Kahlua, and added milk. I tried my best to get Allison to drink it, but she refused. Finally, I thought, what the heck, took the nipple off, unscrewed the cap and turned the bottle up and chugged it!

Does This Fig Leaf Make Me Look Fat?

As I was drinking, I was thinking, *if anyone could see me right now, I would not get the Mother of the Year award!!* I certainly didn't feel like the perfect mother, but after chugging the entire bottle, I didn't CARE!

We pray a lot when we become mothers, or we should! Motherhood is the most rewarding and the most humbling experience in the whole world. In my opinion, after prayer, keeping a sense of humor and being able to laugh at things are the most important things a mother can do to keep things in perspective.

When Allison was about five years old, she came to me and said, "Sean asked me to marry him, but Stephen did, too. I told Sean that I was going to marry Stephen—that I couldn't have millions of husbands." Then she said to me, "Mama, you've had lots of husbands, haven't you? What's a girl to do?" (I married husband number two in 1984.)

Women, I feel, tend to equate our worth as mothers to the behavior and actions of their children—which is very *scary* and the *wrong* thing to do. This is where humor comes to our rescue again. Most mothers have learned that sometimes you just laugh to keep from crying, and hope you've done a good job instilling values. One example of this is when my college-age son came home from Australia, where he had been an exchange student. About a week after he had arrived home, my husband brought me a t-shirt that had been on top of my son's suitcase. I looked at it and on the front it read:

"This is not a beer gut. It's a fuel cell for a sex machine!" I just had to laugh and hope for the beer gut this time (I decided it was the lesser of the evils).

I remember another time laughter carried me through. Allison had ADHD and was, shall I say, very high-maintenance. It took a great deal of energy and patience to parent her. When she was about nine years old, I needed some space and time to myself to regroup after an especially draining day. I told her I was going into my bedroom to be alone for a little while and locked the door. She screamed at me to let her in and pulled on the door, but again I told her that I would be out in a few minutes. Well, it got so quiet that I thought maybe she had gone to her room. Suddenly, I heard this noise, *squeak, squeak, squeak,* and wondered what in the world it was. In a few minutes the entire door came off the hinges. Allison had watched my husband use the Phillips head screwdriver and so she decided that, if I wouldn't open the door, she would just take it off the hinges! There she stood with a big smile on her face. I just sat there in shock. The more I thought about it the funnier it seemed, and I started laughing...especially since the schools were telling me that Allison didn't pay attention and would never learn how to do anything.

A friend told me another humorous story about Motherhood. A neighbor of hers had a little boy in the first grade who was sitting at home one day looking at a book. The mom noticed his hands in his pants and said, "William, what are you doing?" He answered, "Moving it around." The mom said, "Why?" He smiled, "Because it feels excellent." A stern voice boomed, "Please stop and go wash your hands." The little boy then said, "No, Mom. It's my *hobby*!"

A woman I met at a church retreat shared with me how humor certainly helped her deal with her *very* active little four-year-old boy, who was into everything. She told him he needed to just keep Jesus in his heart. He replied, "Mom, I do have Jesus in my heart, the problem is that I have the devil in my head!"

Everyone I've ever talked with has told me how humor and laughter helped them reduce the stress of parenting and keep things in perspective. Children can say the funniest things, but the problem is that most people don't write them down. My daughter-in-law sent me some funny things that my twin grandsons, Alex and Trey, said when they were three years old:

Mommy: "I got too much sun and now I'm sun burnt."
Alex: "Your mommy didn't put sunscream on you?"

Mommy's skin was peeling from the sunburn.
Alex: "Why are you ripping?"

After saying our prayers each night, Trey says, "The Devil not going to get me because I like God!"

My stepson shared a funny line that came from my 3-year-old granddaughter, Lily. She was upset about something and was crying and said, "My eyes are leaking!"

Friends

Family relationships are important. Especially for women, friends provide a special bonding and help us with our self-esteem in many ways. The following quote is so very true.

> *"A friend walks in when the rest of the world walks out."*
> *Anonymous*

I feel that Dinah Shore, a famous singer from "yesteryear," really hit the nail on the head with her thoughts about friends and relationships. She said: *"Trouble is part of your life. If you don't share it, you don't give the person who loves you a chance to love you enough."*

There are seven of us who are lifelong friends. In fact, we call ourselves the Magnificent Seven (ha), and all are from the same small town in South Carolina. We went to Brownie Scouts and Girl Scouts together. Some of us went to Sunday school and church together, to elementary school together, and we all went to high school together. In fact, some of us even went to the same college.

After graduation, we all married and scattered across five states. Our one special gathering spot was Pawley's Island, a coastal island off South Carolina with the proud label, "arrogantly shabby."

We all grew up going to Pawley's Island, because one girl's family owned a wonderful, rambling, weathered house right on the beach. There are so many memories…coating our bodies with baby oil and sunning on the beach and behind the sand dunes…teenagers spending hours putting on make-up and working on new hair-do's, only to have them blown in all directions by the salty sea breeze...going to Pawley's Pavilion, a rough, old building with wooden floors sitting on the marsh, where all the teens went to listen to beach music played by groups like the Tams and the Drifters, and to dance the shag. Years passed and still we all gathered at Pawley's, through marriages, babies, divorces, illnesses, dreams, heartaches, laughter, new marriages, teenagers, children leaving home, children coming home, grandbabies, aging parents, deaths, and our own aging.

This poem, *"The Girls,"* expresses it best:

"The Girls"
The girls of summer, with golden tans
Basking in the sunshine on glistening sands.
The colorful chairs again unfold,
Facing the sea, full of memories of gold.
The radio, spinning memories of the past,
The same ole story with a new cast.
The warm fragrant breeze gently blows,
The talking and laughing never slows.
Taking no notice of the passing years
For a short time putting far away any fears.
Friends, whose sisterly love has endured,
And through all trials has gradually matured.
Stories recounted as though yesterday,
Never losing the humor of girls at play.
The girls of summer have aged with grace,
Love and smiles have sculptured their face.
Distance and time will never give way,
When it is time for the girls to play.

Margie Tolly[6]

SPIRITUAL

Personal Relationship With God

Our personal relationship with God and our Christian walk with Him define who we are and our reason for being. We are all special to Him and have special purposes. Focusing on this builds our self-esteem and self-worth in the proper ways. Many women feel unproductive and unfulfilled, because their whole lives have been centered on either what others can do for them or the belief that they have nothing to offer.

Spiritual Gifts

God gives us all spiritual gifts. Our challenge is to let God show us His plan, to see ourselves as He sees us and open up our hearts and minds to new possibilities. Sometimes this is difficult. Not because God isn't talking to us, but because we aren't listening. Maybe it's that form of selective listening we all know about.

For years I struggled with trying to find my spiritual gifts. I would love to sing and be in the choir, but my singing (squawking) would empty the church. A friend commented that if one Sunday he sang in the choir, by the next week those good Presbyterians that had been there would be good Methodists!! I'm not good at administrative, financial or many other areas, and started thinking that maybe somehow I got left out. I started praying and *listening* and realized that what we enjoy doing and what we do best are God's ways of equipping us to serve Him. Teaching, motivating, writing, listening, and helping people bring out the best in themselves are rewarding to me.

When I first started speaking at women's faith retreats, something happened that made me realize God was leading me in the direction of helping others. I was speaking at a mother-daughter banquet and my topic was "Feeling like a Raggedy Ann in a Barbie World," dealing with trying to have a healthy, Christian self-esteem in a looks-conscious world. After the program, a woman and her adult daughter came by to speak to me. The daughter, who had a lisp and some physical and mental challenges, said, "I'm glad you came tonight. It's hard sometimes because I hear people whispering that I'm not normal. I want to say 'Well, what's normal?'" She hesitated and looked directly into my eyes and said, "You made me feel so pretty tonight." She started walking towards the door and turned and said, "Thank you." I couldn't say a word because I had a lump in my throat the size of my fist. What I wanted to say was, "No...Thank you!"

Finally, I feel that I have found some of my spiritual gifts. Now I just have to find a way to use them. I want to be like the late humor columnist, Erma Bombeck, who said, "When I stand before God at the end of my life, I would hope that I would not have a single bit of talent left and could say, 'I used everything you gave me.'"[7]

The following list represents just some of the areas in which we can use our gifts in our churches and communities. Think about where your passions lie and where you might be most suited.

SPIRITUAL GIFTS: greeter, nursery, cooking, hospital visitation, arts and crafts, women's ministry, usher, vacation Bible school director, financial secretary, church historian, choir, children's choir, band, hand bells, handywoman, shut-in-ministry, missions work, prison ministry, Stephen minister, teacher, leader.

Growing In Faith, Esteem and Purpose

When we doubt ourselves and put ourselves down, we live in small comfort zones. Think of something you feel you aren't good at or are uncomfortable with—public speaking, heights, trying new things, speaking up for yourself. Look at the destructive cycle we create:

- Here are the things we feel we are not good at…
- So we tend to fear them…
- Because we fear them, we avoid them…
- Because we avoid them, we rarely improve…
- Because we rarely improve, here are the things we feel we're not good at!

So many of us fear taking risks and trying things, because we think we might *fail*. I don't know how many times I have beaten myself up mentally because things did not work out the way I wanted or planned. The following quote has really helped me put things in perspective:

> *"It's one thing to experience failure and another to be a failure."*
> Charles Stanley

> *"This thing that we call "failure" is not the falling down, but the staying down."*
> Mary Pickford, actress

If we don't do something to change the destructive cycles we create, nothing will improve, especially our self-esteem. First turn to God for direction, strength and guidance, and then take a risk and decide to change something. Practice does not make *perfect*. Practice does make *permanent*. I know some people who are permanently fearful. You have to practice the RIGHT things. The cycle is broken between fear and avoidance. It's OK to fear something; that's normal and human. What we have to do is make a conscious decision to break out of our comfort zones, even though we are afraid. That's called being brave. Faith is like that, because faith turns negatives into positives.

"Now faith is being sure of what we hope for and certain of what we do not see."
Hebrews 11:1

We never arrive; our lives are journeys. This is true whether we're trying to change habits or grow in faith. An analogy that comes to mind is the airplane. A plane can go in three directions. It can go up and forward. If it's not going in those two directions, it will start to go in the third direction—down. It cannot stand still. I feel the same applies for us. When we stop going forward (learning and growing), we start going down!

"Courage is not the lack of fear. It is acting in spite of it."
Mark Twain

This letter came from a woman in one of my workshops. It's just one more example of opening up to God, taking risks and trying to change our lives:

Food, television and anger were ways I attempted to handle my depression. A broken home and low self-esteem were triggers of my depression. On top of that, I was a customer service rep taking 200, sometimes 300 calls a day. After 3 years, the job began to weigh on me. Following every 3rd or 4th call, all I could do was cry. When I would come home from work, I would go into my room, close the door and watch television in a dark room. On Fridays, when I had a taste for it, I would go by the Pizzeria and order a large vegetarian pizza and consume the entire pie while watching rented movies. The movies placed me in a world of fantasy where I felt accepted, something I did not receive from my *father. I wanted a way out of this depression and to end the cycle of destruction. I asked Christ into my life. Because of allowing God to move into my life, He has allowed me to look to Him for the love I searched for.*

As of today, I feel I've been called into youth ministry. I look forward to sharing God's word and love with youth who, like me, are looking for love in all the wrong places. I also have a new job that I love. My relationship with my father is back on track. I have forgiven him for not being there. The hate I had for him caused the anger and depression I endured, but God allowed me to forgive him.

There are other hurdles I have to cross, but I know God will always be there to see me through. He is why I am here today. My faith in God is everlasting.

Sandra

Self-Esteem Stories

Learn From Your Mistakes—They Become Your Greatest Gifts

Merry,

I came to class today with a heavy heart. I am trying to teach my 13-year-old daughter to discipline her mind, and we argued last night and this morning. As usual, this class was an angel in disguise. I almost didn't come, since I was so distracted, but am grateful that I did. I admire what you are doing and wish you continued success. Thanks so much for today's life lessons!

I am the younger of two daughters of a mother who led by example. She worked in a textile factory for fifty-two years in a small southern town. It was the only job she ever had. Her tenant farmer father refused to allow her to go to college, and she dedicated her life to seeing that my sister and I received a good education.

My sister, three years my senior, was an extremely intelligent young woman who buried her anxiety in books. She was the 100-average, top of the class student with much personal reserve that all 1960's teachers adored. I was expected to follow her intellectual lead and brought home comparable grades, but was much more extroverted and distracted by the world around me.

I attended nursing school with scholarships from the factory that our mother dedicated her working life to and graduated with a B.S. Degree in Nursing. While in college, I met an astonishingly handsome man nine years my senior who was finishing a bachelor's degree. He was unhappily married to a second wife and had two children. Against every rational thought, and realizing that I was making a mistake every step of the way, I married him a few months after college graduation.

In retrospect, I see a depressed man who let opportunity pass him by at several turns along the road of life. I also see two people whose collective presence brought much heartache to each of their lives. As the early years passed, neither of us was earning enough money to move forward. I understood nothing about finances, and landed us in unparalleled debt over the next twenty years with credit cards. I tried to buy my way out of unhappiness. As debt grew and possessions did not, I began to work overtime or at secondary employment to earn more money. His children were getting older, and wanted extra things above the child support he owed. Having my own child was out of the question.

He grew more despondent and more demanding. I worked two jobs, kept the house, cut the four acres of grass every week in the summer, cooked, cleaned, washed the cars, ironed the clothes, etc. None of this suited him. I paid the bills in an effort to keep him from seeing what I spent. Our co-existence continued to deteriorate.

I left, but later went back. Then I got pregnant. My husband's discontent grew, as did mine. His behavior grew more forceful and bullying, yet his contribution to our household was miniscule. He criticized everything I did. Bills escalated, since I tried to give my daughter a normal life. No friends or teachers could visit—we lived in a ramshackled mobile home in an isolated area. When we were home, my husband was in the recliner with the TV on blast, my daughter was in her room watching TV and I was working or in the other tiny bedroom with the door shut, crying and trying to find a way out.

My mother died after an extended illness and her small mill house went up for sale. When it sold, I filed bankruptcy on both my and my husband's behalf, filed for legal separation, and moved out on a workday with the help of friends from my work. This all had to be done in silence since I could not approach my husband. His reaction would have been violent. I had police protection for the first few days, because I feared his reaction.

I did not know until I approached a divorce attorney that I could file for bankruptcy. I had suffered all those years due to financial ignorance. Perhaps those years served as my resolve to move forward.

Working fourteen-hour weekend days and scurrying for a babysitter for my daughter for weekends, I worked in a state facility for the profoundly mentally retarded. It was hard, but my small circle of support was firm.

My daughter is an extremely intelligent young lady, and her mother is devoted to her success in life and determined to see her apply her talents. My sister is an Academic Dean at a state university dedicated to helping people get an education.

Learn from your mistakes—they become your greatest gift. Support other women who need your help. Teach your daughters how to succeed in life. And when you get to Heaven, thank my mother. Her name is Ruby.

Name Withheld

Fulfilling Our Purpose

My name is Tasha, and I am a 32 year-old single parent. My daughter is 11 and my son is 10. I purchased my own home at the age of 27. My daily occupation is a claims associate for an insurance company, but my life occupation (purpose) is to take everything I've learned and help other young women learn how they can make it in life. I am a mentor. For six years now I have taken young women in my home to help teach ways they can overcome their situation no matter what it is. I network with different programs such as Family Outreach and Mental Health to provide housing and other needs. One of my main focuses is to help them realize that they have a purpose and place in life. The best example I give is that you are a domino piece in a picture creation, and basically you have to make sure you are in place to affect the next domino. There is a place in life where you are supposed to be. Don't let circumstances keep you from achieving your goal, whether it is a mental health disability or being a single parent. We can classify anything as a disability to keep us from purpose. Use the situation, whatever it is, as a stepping stone. Don't let it overcome you. Welcome it! Both of my children are honor students, play sports, and also play instruments. I push them to be the best they can be and avoid the mistakes I made. I stay very busy with all this on my plate, but believe it or not these are the best years of my life, because I know I am fulfilling my purpose.

Tasha

Pretty

My sister Kaye is battling breast cancer. We are two girls in a family of ten children and none of us have ever been overly confident about our looks. While Kaye was undergoing chemotherapy, she suffered the usual effects, including the loss of hair. This was especially hard for her and she was always careful to keep her wig on whenever anyone besides myself was around. One day my boyfriend, William, and I went down to visit her and she wanted me to massage her head. We had done this before but only when we were alone. When she asked William if it would bother him to see her without her wig, he said no and she slowly pulled it off. After our visit, as we were pulling out to come home, William turned to me and said, "You know, I never realized until today how pretty your sister is." It was the first time he had ever called her pretty. When I told my sister we both cried.

Michelle

If You Believe In Yourself

There I sat at the age of seventeen, on top of the world, a senior in high school facing my parents. What could it be? My mother is obviously troubled. She says it, "Your senior counselor felt you should not be a nurse because you have poor math skills." I looked around, my reply to my parents, "Well, I don't care." On that day I set my mind and maintained my goal to one day become a Registered Nurse. I had a few setbacks—not math. I quickly learned, don't let what others say you cannot do, stop you from doing what you want to do, no matter how long it takes!!!

Some eighteen years later, I am proud to say, I have been an RN for twelve years. Why? Because I believed something my father always told me to remember— "You have not because you ask not." Doing my best, prayer and assurance from a strong family made the difference. You can achieve— just do it!

Lisa

How Could I Be a Failure?

In all honesty, I feel like I am a failure—my marriage didn't succeed, I have never finished college, I haven't become the person I wanted to be, nor have I accomplished any great feat. One night after work, my three daughters and I arrived home. It was a hectic evening to say the least. The house was a disaster, the dishes were piled high in the sink and laundry was spilling out of the laundry room. We were low on groceries with no milk in the fridge. I wasn't getting paid for a few days yet. To say the least, I was stressed out. We made it through the evening, but I know that the girls could see the pain and stress in my face, not to mention hear it in my voice. I was short with them all night. I wasn't mad at them, but frustrated with my situation. I went into Sophie and Chloe's room to tuck them into bed. I kissed Sophie and told her good night and then went to Chloe. I leaned over to kiss her and she handed me something. It was all the money that she had saved in the last 6 months. It was only about 6 dollars. She then said, "Mom, when you don't have enough money to buy milk, then I will buy it." A huge smile was on her face and I had tears well up in my eyes. Wow, I can hardly tell you the pride in my heart over her unselfishness. I thanked her and told her how proud of her I was, kissed her good night and turned out the light. I then went to tuck my 5-year-old, Tessa, into bed and she said, "Mommy, will you read me a book?" I said, "Not now honey, mommy is feeling real sad, and all I want to do is go to sleep." She then got a big smile on her face and said, "Would you like me to rub your feet?" I felt ashamed of my selfishness and so much love for her.

I guess what I'm saying is that these children keep me going. They are my life support. If I were such a failure, then how is it that they are so amazing? They make my life crazy most of the time, but I would truly be a failure without them in my life.

Laura

My Gift from God—Family and Friends

I was a twenty-three-year-old pregnant wife, separated from her husband, who was living back at home with her mom. I was six and a half months and working two jobs, trying to make sure my unborn child had all the material things that he/she would need. One Saturday I was visiting a friend who wanted to give me a baby shower. On the way home a city worker waved me through an intersection and I was hit in the driver's side by an oncoming car. It slid my car seventy-six feet and turned it 180 degrees, landing tail first in a ditch. I was cut from the car and rushed to the hospital. They sent me home saying I had no broken bones, only cuts and bruises. The next morning I tried to get up and couldn't walk. I was again taken to the hospital Emergency Room (different one) and they checked me over. My right hand was broken, so they sent me to see an orthopedic doctor. I still couldn't walk at this point (I was being carried by my stepfather). The doctor set my hand and put it in a cast and he also found out why I couldn't walk. I had actually broken my pelvis in two places. On top of this, my left elbow had twenty-seven stitches in it. My left leg was messed up, also. The calf muscle was about severed in two and the open gashes were numerous. I was put on complete bed rest for three months until my child was born. I had to depend on my mom for just about everything. I couldn't use my right hand, it was broken, my left was bandaged (stitched elbow) in a bent position. I had a head concussion and a small fracture under my eye. I couldn't walk because of my broken pelvis and couldn't use my left leg because of the calf muscle. I had to depend on friends, family and baby sitters for my well-being. They had to feed me, bathe me, clothe me and let me go to the bedpan (yuck). They kept my spirits up and even helped me financially. I had to use state aid to pay for the birth of my daughter.

My friends ended up getting everything for my daughter. She's now a beautiful sixteen-year-old.
Family and friends are a blessing from God.
Teresa

An Act of Kindness

One day I was working diligently at my computer on a time sensitive project. About 1 PM, I had to abruptly stop my work to drive across town to pick up a key to unlock a training room for a class I was to teach the next morning. I was quite frustrated that there was no other way to have the key available the next day. It would take me over an hour to make the trip to pick up the key. Plus, it was summer in the south and the day was miserably hot and sticky. Nevertheless, I got in my car and started down the interstate to pick up the key.

I had not been on the interstate long when I saw an older gentleman on the side of the road standing by his car, which was undoubtedly broken down. He was wearing a plaid cotton shirt (much like my father would wear in the summer), and he was waving his white handkerchief for help. As the other cars zoomed past, something inside me told me to pull over and offer to help the man.

As I slowed to a stop in front of him, he came over to the car and explained that he and his wife were on the way to an "important" doctor's appointment when their car broke down. I offered to drive them to the appointment and they gratefully accepted the offer.

As we drove down the interstate, he explained to me that he was stricken with lung cancer and the appointment was a cancer treatment. He told me that the prognosis was not good. His wife sat quietly in the back seat, but I could sense that she was very worried about him. He told me that he had been waving for help back on the interstate for about twenty minutes and he was worried about making his appointment on time. He did not want to miss it.

At exactly 2:25 PM I arrived at the hospital where he had a 2:30 appointment. We said our goodbyes and God Bless You. I offered to drive them back home, but they felt confident that someone would come to pick them up and help with the car situation. I gave them my business card with my name and phone number, just in case they did need some help. Then I left them at the hospital and continued on my journey to pick up the key.

On the drive back home, I realized that perhaps the reason I had to stop my work that afternoon and get in the car and drive across town, wasn't really about the key at all. Maybe I was part of a bigger plan. Maybe I was supposed to help this man and his wife. Whether there was a greater purpose or not, I felt so much better because I had stopped and taken the opportunity to help someone.

Later that year, in December, I received a Christmas card in the mail from a name I didn't recognize. It was from the man's wife. She wrote that she had found my card in her husband's wallet sometime after this death from the lung cancer. She went on to say how she appreciated my kindness on the hot summer day. Of all the cards and letters that I've received over the years, I don't think any have meant as much to me as this one—knowing that I really helped someone.

Donna

Old, Old Age

Wouldn't it be consoling if we could do as the Grecian ladies? They count their age from the time of their marriage, not from their birth. I don't know what the unmarried do.

Even though it is a shock the first time we are called "old," I have to admit that 86 is old. But since we are here and have aged with family and friends at a steady pace, it is comforting that we are together.

I'm of the same opinion as Erma Bombeck. She wrote that because she and her husband had been married for so long, they must stay together, as they needed each other to finish sentences. So it is. Have you noticed?

I have tried, but it is a difficult attainment to grow old gracefully; however, I have grown older happily. And I have reached maturity.

All of us know that our future path is a mystery but there is abiding peace and joy in the years of the past. And I do like to tell you again and again all about that. Our children, grandchildren and great grandchildren receive all the credit for the happiness they give us.

Do you realize that the first 80 years are the hardest? The second 80 years create a succession of birthday celebrations. At 80 you always have the perfect excuse when you don't want to do something. You just say no thanks.

It's your second childhood and everybody "understands." Family and friends expect you to become hard of hearing, the brain to soften, and your pace to lose its speed. Actually they are surprised that you can walk and talk sensibly about some things besides your aches and pains.

But everybody forgives you for everything. They treat you with profound respect for just having lived so long.

You are old.

Maybe life begins at 80!

Mary Janet

Our True Feelings

My name is Monica and I attended a class on self-esteem by Merry Taylor. During this class we discussed our true feelings about life and what we were going through. Needless to say, I left the class in tears, because I could see it in writing that I was severely depressed. After class, I called my doctor and made an appointment. When I got to the doctor, I could not bring myself to talk to him, so I just gave him my workbook from class. He was so kind and he didn't say anything. He put me on medicine for depression. This medicine really helped me have a better outlook on life. Soon after, about 4 or 5 months, I was diagnosed with cancer. I thought my world had come to an end. I was 34 years old, married, mother of 2 young children and building my dream home, and now I had cancer. My husband kept the faith when I lost it. After I was mad, upset and wanted to give up, I remembered to have faith. I prayed and asked for help again with my health. God answered my prayers. I went through 4 months of chemotherapy (that I hated) and I am now in remission. God promised me good health, and that is what I received.

I can now sit and think about how I came out of my depression and cancer. I have a better outlook on life.

Thank you, Mrs. Taylor, for putting me on the right track to getting my life together.

Monica

To God Be the Glory

In 1970, when I was a senior in college, I felt that God was calling me to be a missionary. Instead, on February 18, 1970, I had a complete nervous breakdown, and what I've learned over the years is that God was calling me to represent the mentally ill the best way I can.

In the forty-one years since my psychotic breakdown, I've grown closer to my loving heavenly father by worshiping Him from 4am to 6am.

Joni Eareckson Tada said it best in 1987, "People with disabilities are God's best visual to demonstrate who he really is. His power shows up best in weakness."

I want to thank the MD's and residents in medical school who treated me and then thanked me for teaching them so much by studying my mental illness.

Margaret

CHAPTER FOUR

And Adam Said, "Eve Honey, Have You Seen My Rib?"
(Male/Female Communication and Relationships)

"So God created man in His own image, in the image of God He created him; male and female He created them."
Genesis 1:27

"It's easy to understand love at first sight, but how do we explain love after two people have been looking at each other for years?"
Author Unknown

News Flash—Men and Women Are Different!

In case you haven't noticed, men and women are different! God made us that way, and it was part of His plan. We were made to be helpmates and to complement each other.

Remember the old saying, *opposites attract*? That may be true, but opposites can also *irritate*! This can become a big source of stress in marriages, relationships, and in our lives in general. A friend said that her husband recently told her, "It never ceases to amaze me how different we are!" Nowhere are these differences more apparent than in the area of communication. Men and women have very different communication styles. Neither is right or wrong, just different. Although not all men fit into one category or all women into another, overall there are *big* differences. The challenge is to understand these differences and use them to build strong Christian relationships and marriages.

So, what are some of these differences? We're generalizing, but here are a few of them. Most men talk to give information or details; they talk about things, sports, business, and usually not about people. They want to solve and fix problems, and don't often ask for help or directions (whether it's how to repair something or directions to someplace).

"I have yet to hear a man ask for advice on how to combine marriage and a career."

Gloria Steinem

What about women? Most talk to socialize, get information and gain rapport. We talk about people, feelings and relationships, not things. And we *will* ask for directions.

A woman told me about her husband and her hardwood floors. One day she noticed some spots on them and mentioned it to her husband at dinner. The next afternoon she came home from work and her husband was beaming. He took her into the dining room and showed her the floors and said, "Honey, look what I did. I put something on them and it took out the water spots." The wife noticed that the places were turning a weird color and asked her husband what he had used. He told her and she exclaimed, "Sam, you used *that* on them? Why? Didn't you read the directions? You can't use that on hardwood floors!" "No," he hollered back. "Why did I need to read the directions? I just did what I thought would fix it."

Men focus on one thing at a time. Ann told me she was going to a church circle meeting one evening and asked her husband to watch the children. When she came home, the dinner dishes were still on the table. She was a little miffed and asked her husband why he had not done the dishes. His response was, "You didn't ask."

Another way men and women frequently differ is in their handling of criticism. I have been in business meetings and watched men practically come to blows, holler and curse at each other, and then say, "Hey, Joe, it's lunchtime. Let's get a bite to eat." Then they would proceed to go to lunch together. You are *not* going to see many women do that!

Everybody has stress, but overall men and women deal with stress differently. Men compartmentalize; they do not become energized by constantly processing life. In fact, it drains them of energy. When was the last time you heard a man say, "I feel the need to talk and get in touch with my feelings"? Yeah, right. So, what do most men do? They retreat to their compartments—sports, computers, music, etc. I love the following quote and believe it is true:

"When women are depressed they either eat or go shopping. Men invade another country."

Elayne Boosler

Women, on the other hand, tend to interconnect with other people (especially family members), feel more of their pain, and therefore feel more stress. Linda reflects, "As wives, mothers, sisters and daughters, we often find ourselves trying to change things and people for the better. We have so many good ideas, if they would only listen. My husband has told me repeatedly (usually in a loud voice), 'Linda, I AM NOT YOU!' To which I want to reply, 'WHY NOT?' It would make things so much easier."

I often compare women to sponges, because we soak up others' feelings. I also think women tend to feel more day-to-day stress because of our emotional ties as wives, mothers, caretakers, employees and friends. For some reason, women feel it's our job to make sure everyone is happy. And when someone is not happy (which, of course, is a great deal of the time) women take on the pain and stress. So, ironically, those very traits or qualities that make women good nurturers also cause us to feel more stress and therefore neglect caring for our own needs.

Talking about these feelings and problems helps most of us deal with our stress. Women want husbands to notice feelings and talk, especially when we think men have done something to hurt our feelings. Most men just want to avoid talking. So what do women do? Whatever it takes to get noticed: rattle pots, slam frying pans on the stove and shut drawers so loudly you could hear the silverware clang a mile away! Finally, our *subtle* gestures are noticed and husbands ask what's wrong. Of course we say, "Nothing." They say, "OK," and we walk off and burst into tears! You see, men take us at face value when we say nothing is wrong. In our minds they're supposed to *know* what's wrong. We *shouldn't* have to tell them!

It's taken me years to get to the point where I can express my needs and feelings and not expect a person to read my mind. When I hear women in my workshops talking about how their husbands should know how they're feeling or know they need help, I tell them that they are being unfair to their husbands, and that they should be specific and communicate their needs.

There was a commercial on television that I loved. Whoever wrote it must be a student of the differences between men and women. It's a beer commercial in which all the men in a bar are saying, "How ya doin'*?*" to each other. Everyone answers with, "How ya doin'?" One man walks in and is greeted with, "How ya doin'?" and the man replies, "Well, not too good, let me tell..." and goes on to talk about his feelings. All the other men in the bar have stunned looks on their faces, because no one has ever responded that way and they don't know what to say or how to handle it.

We can also tell the differences in men and women in the greeting cards they send to each other. Several years ago my son and daughter-in-law sent me a birthday card that made me laugh out loud, because it was so true to form. On the outside of the card was written—*Happy birthday from the both of us. We each wanted to wish you happy birthday in our own unique way, so we bought two cards*. It opened up and there was a small insert with flowers on the front and all these wonderful sentimental words, and it was signed by my daughter-in-law. Below was another insert that had a picture of a duck with his tongue hanging out, and opened up and said, "*Yeah, yeah, whatever.*" Can you guess whom that was from?

A woman gets a compliment on her dress and she will probably say, "This old dress? It is so old and just doesn't fit me as well anymore and..." and then continue putting herself down. A man gets a compliment on a tie that looks nice and he will probably say, "Yeah."

In general, most men tend to hold feelings in...what I call the stoic mode. When they're angry, they frequently shout or swear. Women want to talk about feelings when we're angry and tend to cry more. Personally I think there would be fewer heart attacks in men if they would cry more. Sometimes a good cry can be very therapeutic.

Also, there are some words or phrases you will probably never hear a woman say. One is "*Pull my finger.*" Another is "*I'll just pee outside.*"

Does This Fig Leaf Make Me Look Fat?

While sitting in the lab room of a doctor's office watching people weigh in before seeing my physician, it dawned on me that men and women view stepping on the scales differently. The women, even the thin ones, would say, "Do I have to?" or, "Oh, no, I don't want to weigh; I've gained some weight." They would take off their shoes, sweaters, vests, and bracelets... anything that *could* and *would* come off. The men, no matter what size, just stepped on the scales, smiled, and then walked off, seemingly oblivious to the numbers on the scales.

Another area where men and women are different is in the area of hair color. Men that are graying are called "distinguished." Women that are graying are usually perceived as "old" or "matronly." Most men don't care that they are graying, and just accept it. However, most women fight it like the plague—even in death. Let me explain. While waiting in a hair salon, I overheard a woman telling the stylist she needed hair color because her roots were showing. The stylist then told her of a conversation she had with a family member of a recently deceased woman whose obvious gray roots needed color before her burial. The stylist said she told the family member that hair coloring wouldn't "take" on a dead person, because the process needed body heat. The woman sitting in the chair sat up straight and exclaimed, "Gracious, I didn't know that. Guess I'm going to have to plan my death and funeral around my roots!" We all started laughing.

There are two things that I'm absolutely convinced are male genetic traits. One is refusing to ask for directions when driving and the other is absolute control of the remote for the television. Most women I talk to say their husbands get wild-eyed looks on their faces when they get remotes in their hands. And then it starts—the channel surfing. I have twin grandsons and the remote is one of their favorite toys. Need I say more?

Linda talks about the gender differences in her family: "My four children grew up in basically the same environment. They had the same mother, father, race, religion and socio-economic background. Yet with all they had in common, the boys and girls were so different. The two boys couldn't be in the same room without knocking each other down or having a body noise contest. The girls weren't so physical, but they would scream insults at each other when one would try to wear the other's clothes to high school (without asking, of course): 'You can wear it, but you look fat in it'... to which her sister would quickly retort, 'I don't care! I got in the advanced classes on my own; Mom had to talk to the counselors to get you in.'" What differences!

One of the areas where men and women differ most is sex and their approach to it. Billy Crystal summed it up pretty well with this quote: *"Women have to have a reason for sex, men just have to have a place!"* God made us different (and thank goodness for that), but those differences can be challenges and sources of tension and stress for wives and husbands.

Men are visually stimulated. By that I mean—*most men look at women.* They just do. I've had a lot of women tell me that their husbands' looking at other women caused anger and stress for them. I think as most women age we realize it's not the first look that we have to worry about...that's normal... but it's the second, third or fourth. The following is so true.

> **HOW TO IMPRESS A WOMAN:** compliment her, cuddle her, kiss her, caress her, love her, tease her, comfort her, protect her, hug her, hold her, spend money on her, dine her, buy things for her, listen to her, stand by her, go to the ends of the earth for her.
> **HOW TO IMPRESS A MAN: SHOW UP NAKED (and bring food)!**[1]

While there's a lot of truth to the above humorous look at what makes men and women feel amorous, Linda and her husband have a few ideas to add, garnered from many years of marriage (and mistakes). For the guys, Linda suggests that you consider folding clothes, emptying the dishwasher, or bathing the children—cheerfully and without being asked! You may never have considered that to be foreplay, but give it a try and you may be surprised by her reaction! For the ladies, Linda's husband suggests noticing (even *looking* for) things he does well and thanking him for the good job, instead of offering critical remarks or "the look"—especially in front of others! He also appreciates it when Linda prepares breakfast before he leaves for work on the days that she's not rushing out the door to teach. Says Linda, "It took us a while to figure this out and *choose* to do these little things for one another without resentment, but the change in our relationship and openness with each other has been dramatic since we made these choices."

What Men and Women Say—and What They Mean

In life, viewpoints, and in conversation, men and women tend to interpret things differently. You may not agree with all of the following anecdotes. Just think about them and laugh a little.

* * * * * * *

Offer a man a choice between a beautiful, scantily clad woman and a gooey chocolate dessert and he's going to choose—the woman!

Offer a woman a choice between a gooey, hot fudge brownie covered with chocolate sauce and a handsome man and she's going to say, "I can't decide. Do I want pecans or cool whip, walnuts or sauce on my brownie?"

* * * * * * *

Does This Fig Leaf Make Me Look Fat?

A man and woman have a few angry words. The woman puts her hand on the man's arm and he starts thinking—*Oh, let's get amorous and that will make everything better.* A man puts his hand on the woman and she's thinking—*Don't you dare touch me. That's the last thing I want. Talk to me.*

* * * * * * *

A husband and wife are at a high school reunion. An old flame of the wife walks up and she introduces him to her husband. The husband is thinking—*Yeah, yeah, hurry up and let's go home so I can watch the ballgame.*

At the same reunion an old flame of the husband walks up, and the wife starts thinking—*Humph, what a hussy. Look at those dark roots in her hair, and that skirt, so short, makes her look dumpy. And those thighs—how could he have liked her?*

* * * * * * *

A wife says to her husband one Saturday, "Let's have some fun this morning." He starts thinking—*Thanks honey for suggesting I play golf with the guys, or ALL-right, let's head for the bedroom.*

The husband says one Saturday morning, "Let's have some fun this morning." She starts thinking—*He wants to go to the mall. I saw the cutest dress at the store and shoes are on sale also and...*

* * * * * * *

A husband and wife are talking about saving money so they can buy something for the house. The husband is thinking—*Man, that new gas grill with all the attachments is just what we need.*

Does This Fig Leaf Make Me Look Fat?

The wife is thinking—*We need new curtains for the bedroom, new carpet for the den and a new sofa.*

* * * * * * *

A husband and wife are looking at a photo album and see pictures of themselves twenty-five years ago. The husband turns to his wife and asks her if he's changed that much. The wife answers, "Honey, you look better now than you did then." She's thinking—*Well, you're bald and you've gained 50 pounds; but I don't want to hurt your feelings, so I'll make you feel good.*

The wife asks, "Have I changed that much in twenty-five years?" The husband says, "Well, your hair is gray now and you've gained forty or so pounds, but other than that you look pretty good for your age." (Let me comment on this one. He might say that *one* time, but if he's smart, after that he will lie!)

* * * * * * *

A wife has a new dress, models it for her husband, asks him how he likes it, and he says, "It's nice, but I think you look better in dresses that have shoulder pads." He means—*I like it fine, but you look better in dresses that have shoulder pads.*

She's thinking—*You think I look awful, and that I'm fat, and that I'm not pretty anymore, and…..*

* * * * * * *

The husband comes home from a church basketball game with four stitches in his nose. His wife hollers at him, gives him a fit and says, "I told you not to play; I knew this was going to happen." She means—*I love you and wouldn't know what to do if you got hurt really bad.*

The wife comes home from a tennis match with a sprained ankle and the husband says, "Must have been a great match." He means—*Must have been a great match and I hope you beat the fool out of them. Great playing.*

* * * * * * *

Building Better Communication—Where to Turn First

We can laugh at the differences between men and women, but communication problems can cause stress, heartaches and destroy relationships.

What do we do or where do we turn first to build better communication and better relationships? To God. We're just fooling ourselves if we think we're strong enough to handle all our problems without His help.

> *"Unless the Lord builds the house,*
> *its builders labor in vain..."*
> *Psalm 127:1*

Instead of keeping feelings, frustrations and fears bottled up, or blowing up at spouses, pray and talk to God. He always listens and will give us direction. As we begin to talk with God about our problems, we start to examine our own self-talks, and open ourselves up to changing our lives and ourselves. The following letter came to me from a woman who had been in several of my workshops.

Dear Merry,

It's been amazing, but not really so, that in the past few months I have heard the things I've needed to hear, read the things I've needed to read, and met the people I've needed to meet. I say it's not really so amazing because I believe that life is not mysterious—things are meant to be. I'm just glad it was finally time for me to have my eyes, ears, and soul open when these things came along.

Anyway, I want to thank you for presenting some old thoughts in new ways and for exposing me to some new thoughts; for allowing me the opportunity to listen and start regaining control of my life and emotions. You happened along during the hardest one-and-a half years of my life. By February I had allowed myself to slide all the way to the bottom. Luckily, during that time many things you said stayed with me: about faith, prayer, self-talk tapes, the importance of pleasant diversions, and facing our "demons" with truth were the most significant. Although you didn't spend much time on the last issue, I heard it loud and clear. You showed me the starting place I was looking for.

In February, I gave up ownership of my husband's problems, confronted some of my own demons, and decided it was time to get help. I realize now that what you described as my thirst for knowledge was a need for direction—and it has been coming from all angles. Not even a week after you got me started thinking about my life and truth, I read an article about self-disclosure and the power of truth. That really made me re-open my eyes. Then, reading the book **You Just Don't Understand—Women and Men in Conversation**, opened my ears. Again, I thought of you. Now I realize my husband has many of the "typical male" communication traits and I recognize his communication for what it is. Finally, I had the incredible experience of hearing Tony Campola, a Christian motivational speaker. It was inevitable that my soul be re-awakened.

This may seem like an irrelevant out-pouring to you, but it isn't. It's a thank you. I have experienced a real awakening in the past four months. Thank you. What you do really does *matter. You do make a difference to those of us who are ready to listen. Keep talking.*

Sincerely,

Name Withheld

So the first step is putting Christ in the center of a marriage. What's next? The next step is to take a hard, honest look at yourself. Overall, men's and women's communication styles are *simply* different, with neither being right or wrong. I read somewhere that Ruth Graham, wife of evangelist Billy Graham, once said, "*It is my job to love Billy. It is God's job to make him good.*"

We cannot change the other person, and we are not responsible for his/her life. We *are* responsible for our part. We've laughed at some of these differences, but in reality, not all men fall into one category and all women into another. The key is to know ourselves. For example, even though I'm a woman, I have a tendency to withdraw and not talk about things and feelings. My husband, on the other hand, wants to talk things out. He has helped me open up my feelings and learn to talk and share. Each partner in a relationship has to work on those things that reduce stress and help make a marriage successful. Here are some of them.

SHARED SPIRITUAL VALUES

I believe the saying, "Couples that pray together, stay together." If a man and woman share the same spiritual values, read the Bible together, and pray for their marriage and each other, they are putting their priorities in the right order...God first and each other second. From my experience these marriages have more of a chance of succeeding.

COMMITMENT

"One advantage of marriage is that, when you fall out of love with him or he falls out of love with you, it keeps you together until you fall in again."

Judith Viorst

This involves the mindset that the marriage or relationship is a priority, and hard work is necessary to make it succeed. I've actually heard women say, "Well, everyone else is getting married, so guess I'll go ahead and marry Sam. If it doesn't work out, I can always get a divorce." Marriages don't always work out, but if we go into marriage with the "throw-away or disposable" attitude, it won't stand much of a chance of lasting.

There have been times in my marriage when things got so hectic with family responsibilities, demands and problems that I just wanted to run away. It reminds me of something I once heard, *"You show me a woman who says she has never fantasized about getting in her car and leaving home, and I'll show you a woman who doesn't know how to drive!"* How true. Maybe it's tenacity or determination that keeps a marriage together, or maybe it's just that we don't have anywhere else to go!

ACCEPTANCE

Those little things that you love so much about a person when dating can start to wear thin on the nerves later. After hearing the same story about a million times, or the same joke over and over, it's easy to become critical and impatient. Personality traits that seemed cute might not seem as *cute* later. Accepting is just that....it's about give and take.

A young man in a class recently was talking about how different he and his wife are. Then he remarked, "We make a good team. What I'm not good at she is, and what she's not good at I am. We're good together." I think this young man has the right idea; maybe it's about complementing each other to make a strong team. Benjamin Franklin may have hit the nail on the head when he said, *"Keep your eyes wide open before marriage—half shut afterward."*

If you can't do that, how can you expect your spouse to? The Bible addresses acceptance in Romans 15:7, *"Accept one another, then, just as Christ accepted you, in order to bring praise to God."*

RESPECT

The best way to explain respect is to give two examples of lack of respect:

- A husband and wife are at a party and, within everyone's sight, he flirts with another woman the entire evening and totally ignores his wife
- A wife makes hurtful, degrading or cutting remarks about her husband

I knew a man who behaved this way for years in his marriage, and also knew a woman who threw herself at men and belittled her husband. You could see their spouses withdrawing and becoming resentful and bitter. This kind of behavior literally eats away at marriages or relationships. Both of these marriages ended in divorce. Respect is when you think about your spouse, and how your behavior will affect him/her.

ENCOURAGEMENT

In a marriage relationship a spouse should be built up—not put down. Walls start to go up and resentments build if all you receive from your spouse is criticism. There are going to be differences of opinion and unmet expectations, but there is a difference between attacking the problem and attacking the *person*. Everyone needs encouragement. It can change a person's life and a couple's relationship. I knew a woman who was shy and reserved and tended to put herself down. Her husband, however, constantly built her up and encouraged her to use her gifts and talents. Not only did she begin to feel better about herself, but their relationship grew stronger as well.

The Bible talks about how vital it is to encourage and appreciate the one you love and to TELL him. Song of Songs 2:1-2 says, *"I am a rose of Sharon, a lily of the valley (Beloved)... Like a lily among thorns is my darling among the maidens (Lover)."* The Life Application Study Bible says that the rose of Sharon and lily of the valley were flowers that were very common in Israel. The young woman in these verses was comparing herself to them, saying she was nothing special. But Solomon said, "You are very special, a lily among thorns." I wonder how many people get so complacent in their relationships that they don't say, "I appreciate and love you."

COMMUNICATION

> *"My wife says I never listen to her, at least I think that's what she said."*
> *Author Unknown*

This doesn't mean your communication styles have to be the same. What it does mean, however, is that you don't always put the responsibility on the other person. If we reach out and try to understand other people first, and try to meet them halfway, that encourages them to respond to us. Listen and listen some more. Many men think women talk them to death. That's the quickest way to kill listening and communication. Don't just listen to words; listen for meaning. Don't expect the other person to read your mind; be specific about feelings and use "I" statements. Instead of, "You hurt my feelings," say, "My feelings are hurt because of..." or "This is the way I feel." Also, we need to *think* before we speak. A woman in one of my classes summed it up pretty well. She said, "The first thought that pops into your head is an impulse and you do not have any control over that. But your second thought can, and should, be controlled. Guess when most of us open our mouths?"

Another analogy I heard is that communication is like toothpaste. Once you squeeze the toothpaste out—it's out. If you try to put it back into the tube, it will just make a big mess. Words are like that. Once they are out you can try to take them back, but it usually makes a big mess. How true! Good communication involves effort and practice, patience and prayer. James 1: 19 addresses listening with the familiar verse, *"My dear brothers, take note of this: Everyone should be quick to listen, slow to speak and slow to become angry..."*

COMPROMISE

"Marriage is an alliance entered into by a man who can't sleep with the window shut, and a woman who can't sleep with the window open."
George Bernard Shaw

In my marriage, compromise could best be illustrated when my husband agreed to play bridge in a couple's bridge club once a month, if I would help him bale hay for our horses by driving the truck. It's also important to be positive and upbeat in the situation. If we complain the entire time about having to compromise, and fuss about how much we don't enjoy the activity, it takes away all the pleasure for the other person.

People are going to have different interests and desires. It only becomes a problem when the relationship becomes very one-sided, and one partner starts to resent it. Another word that comes to mind is involvement. I don't feel that we have to be involved in all our spouse's interests; but when there is little or no involvement or interest in anything they are doing, from work to hobbies, it creates gaping holes in the relationship.

During a stress management workshop a man told the group that before working on getting their jobs straightened out, they needed to examine their marriages and make sure they are strong. When asked what he meant, the man replied, "Well, I had been so busy with my career and working long hours that when our children left home, my wife and I realized we were living with strangers! It had been so long since we did anything together, we had to develop common interests again."

FORGIVENESS

> "Marriage is three parts love and seven parts forgiveness of sins."
> Langdon Mitchell

Forgiveness is tough! You know it's the Christian thing to do, but it's still difficult. However, if you can't forgive, you start to build resentments that are like walls. They get bigger and bigger as you add more resentment. Walter Wangerin, in his book *As for Me and My House*, brings out the real issue in forgiveness. He says, "In order to forgive your spouse—so to heal the broken relationship—first forget your spouse. The primary relationship is between you and God; what happens there will affect what happens in your household. First, it is you and God alone."

When you look at forgiveness in this light, it prevents forgiveness from becoming simply getting even, keeping score, or "you owe me." It just cleans the slate. Plus, it's good to cultivate a short memory! [2]

I read a story about Clara Barton, the founder of the American Red Cross. She was reminded one day of a vicious deed that someone had done to her years before. She chose to act as if she had never heard of the incident. "Don't you remember it?" her friend asked. "No," came Barton's reply. "*I distinctly remember forgetting it.*" Wouldn't life be less stressful if we had that same mindset about forgiveness?

LAUGHTER AND HUMOR

I feel very strongly that when laughter goes out of a marriage, trouble follows. When a couple is dating, usually laughing and teasing and joking are very much a part of the relationship. Fun and intimacy are present. To me, when laughter stops, it's like a candle going out. Sharing laughter is one of life's joys, and making others laugh is a gift.

In the book *Good Marriage*, Judith Wallerstein and Sandra Blakesee talk about the critical role humor can play in a relationship. Couples who described marriages as "happy" repeatedly referred to the laughter shared between them. [3]

What I've observed in strong marriages is that these couples face differences with a sense of humor and are able to laugh at themselves.

I have a friend who started complaining about her husband. First she said he didn't give her enough money and that he was too possessive. Then she fussed that he wasn't attentive enough, and that he didn't get involved enough in making decisions. She always seemed to find something wrong and rarely focused on finding something right. I tried to be a good friend and listen, gently trying to guide her to the positives. At one point I was concerned that their marriage would not last. Months went by and, I'm not sure what happened, but their relationship started blooming again. When we had lunch, she told me she realized that she had overlooked a lot of her husband's good qualities, and discovered much of her unhappiness had been with *herself*. Then with a smile she said to me, "Also, he still makes me laugh. I can be having a bad day and he will do something crazy and funny just to make me feel better."

Laughter and humor have certainly played important roles in helping my husband and me get through some very tough times. We used to laugh and say that if one of us left the marriage, that person had to take the children—all five of them! What a way to keep a marriage intact.

During a particularly difficult period with our youngest daughter, a family counselor told us that marriages often end in divorce when couples are not united in handling stressful situations involving their children. After praying and talking together, laughing together was probably the next best thing that helped us through those difficult situations.

FRIENDSHIP

> *"This is my lover, this is my friend,*
> *O daughters of Jerusalem."*
> Song of Songs 5:16

The Life Application Study Bible explains that in this verse the girl calls Solomon her "friend," and that in healthy marriages lovers are also good friends. Too often people are driven into marriages by the exciting feelings of love and passion before they take the time to develop deep friendships. Friendship takes time, but it makes a love relationship much deeper and more satisfying.

I've heard women say that they knew people who had perfect marriages. Perfect marriages do not exist, because people make up marriages, and people aren't perfect. You may look at other relationships and wish yours was like that, but it's a big mistake to compare. You never know what's going on in that "perfect marriage." I knew a couple years ago that everyone thought had the perfect marriage. They seemed to be so happy. To my shock and surprise, they announced they were getting a divorce. What I found out was that this couple was living a lie. Both husband and wife had been miserable for years, but for social and financial reasons, they just went through the motions.

Sometimes a person looks for that "perfect" individual when trying to meet the opposite sex. A woman in one of my seminars told me that she had just gone through a divorce and was ready to start meeting people. She joined one of those popular on-line match-making services and filled out a three-page outline of the character traits she was looking for in a man. Several days later a summary came to her that said there was *no match* for the man she was looking for; he didn't *exist*! She laughed and decided she might have to tone down her search for the "perfect" man and try for something a little more realistic.

Something that's not mentioned often when talking about marriage is neglect. A relationship is like a garden or flowerbed: if attention is not given to it, weeds start to gradually take over and the garden just dies or withers away because of neglect. We've all seen marriages like that; attention is given to the children, jobs, clubs, and church, but not to each other.

Phyllis Diller shared her thoughts on marriage when she once said, *"Never go to bed mad. Stay up and fight."* [4] While I'm not advocating fighting, I do agree with Ephesians 4:26-27, *"... Do not let the sun go down while you are still angry, and do not give the devil a foothold."* Resentments start to build and can eventually destroy a relationship.

During one class several women were talking about marriage. A woman said that at night when she and her husband were watching TV, she would get up and make him a snack and bring it to him. Another woman in the class said she wouldn't "wait" on her husband like that. The woman then replied, "I do it because I want to. He does things for me; it's not all one-sided, but not always balanced either. If you're looking for balance, then you're KEEPING SCORE."

The bottom line is that every marriage is different, the stresses are different, communication styles are different, and both the man and woman in that relationship have to find what works for them. *We* may not understand why people stay together. What matters is that *they* know!

My husband tells the humorous story of an old country couple who had been married forever. The man had been a farmer, but was now retired and raised chickens. He was gruff and ornery and didn't pay much attention to his wife, Sarah. As a young man in high school, Ashley (my husband) did odd jobs for the old man and often ate breakfast there. He said that every morning Mr. Jones would sit and eat his grits, without saying a word to his wife, until he wanted something. The ritual was always the same. "Sarah," he would bellow out. "Bring me some *goop* (grape jelly) for my grits." Ashley said the man's wife would drop what she was doing, which was usually cleaning or washing, walk into the kitchen, open the door to the old refrigerator, take out the grape jelly, walk over to the table and spoon some grape jelly on her husband's grits. Then she would walk off without saying a word. Ashley said that not once in all the time he ate breakfast there did the old man get up and get his own *goop*. Why did she do it? Women today (including Linda and myself) might have a problem understanding, but when my husband asked his mother why she thought Sarah stayed with Mr. Jones, she just smiled and said, "She loves him."

"They say love is blind....and marriage is an institution. Well, I'm not ready for an institution for the blind just yet."
Mae West

Sometimes, however, relationships and marriages just do not work. If you've given the relationship everything you've got, gone to counseling and prayed to God, you may find that you just have to pick up the pieces of your life and move on. Sometimes that includes dealing with anger and, for many people, hate. However, Lewis Smedes, author of *Forgive and Forget*, says there is a big difference between anger and hate:

> *We must not confuse hate and anger. It is hate and not anger that needs healing. Anger is a sign that we are alive and well. Hate is a sign that we are sick and need to be healed. Healthy anger drives us to do something to change what makes us angry; anger can energize us to make things better. Hate does not want to change things for the better; it wants to make things worse.* [5]

During a class several women were having a discussion about how broken relationships can play havoc with self-esteem. They all agreed that by letting God into your life, and letting go of hate, you can move forward and have a healthy self-esteem.

Marriage and Communication Stories

Opposites

Jay comes from a family with three boys and I come from a family of three girls. When there is a family gathering at his folks' house, we talk about only sports or politics (my poor mother-in-law). When my parents have a gathering, we discuss our latest buys at the mall, new recipes, or what's new in the lives of our children (my poor father). Jay and I are total opposites in the way we do things in life. He's a night owl; I'm up at the crack of dawn. He's a procrastinator; I'm a "do it now" kind of person. He's a thinker; I'm a reactor. Yes, our 27 years of marriage prove that opposites do attract. The few items we do agree upon are the things that we feel have held our marriage together. We both hate tomatoes and neither of us wants custody of the children.

Our marriage started out on a humorous note. When Jay proposed to me, he first handed me a ring box that held a 4-carat diamond. I knew right away that that was a joke, because we were both college students and I knew how tight Jay was with a buck. After I threw that box at him, he retrieved another box, which held my real ring...a MUCH, much smaller ring (The first one was a cubic zirconium). I kept the second one, but have often wondered if I should have held out for the first one.

Our first year of marriage was probably the most traumatic for the two of us. The first time the in-laws came for a visit, I insisted that Jay go to the corner grocery store to pick up an extra package of toilet paper. His brother had arrived early and volunteered to go with him. At the time it was popular to have toilet paper the color of your bathroom, so I sent Jay and his brother out with specific directions to bring back green toilet paper. Not a hard task, right? It is a more difficult task if you are color-blind. I had sent not one, but two color-blind people to pick out green toilet paper. Neither of the men mentioned this when I asked them to go.

Does This Fig Leaf Make Me Look Fat?

It could have been because they sensed how nervous I was already with my in-laws coming for their first meal. So, they proceeded to the store and picked up what they believed to be green toilet paper. After thinking over the situation and how much flack they might catch if they came back with the wrong color (remember we were newlyweds), they walked up to an older woman and asked her if the toilet paper was green. The woman hesitated and then replied, "Sure it is." At this point they continued to the check-out line. The older woman saw them in line and approached them saying, "You do realize that the toilet paper is really blue." When she saw the shocked look on their faces, she realized that it had not been a college fraternity prank they were pulling and assisted them in finding the green toilet paper. Thank goodness the colored toilet paper has been done away with or, our marriage might have been down the toilet.

I guess Jay and I laugh at ourselves a lot to ease the tension of our weaknesses. Jay knows that I am horrible with names, so anytime we are going to a function I spend the time on the road quizzing him on the name of John's wife, or the names of the Thompsons' children. When I get started on my non-ending school day stories his favorite line is, "I'm afraid you greatly overestimate the depth of my concern." In other words, these stories bore me. And of course there is the whole Sunday School thing. Yes, I hate coming to Sunday School when Jay teaches, because I know my life will be put on display and I can do nothing about it but sit quietly and listen. I really don't care what he says about us, I just don't want to have to listen to it. However, we have even turned that into a family joke. If I am not dressed for church, the kids now ask if Dad is teaching.

Cynthia

Got To Sleep Sometime

Being a retired state trooper, I have seen and heard just about everything, but this story is one of the most unusual. My mother told me it was indeed true and happened back in the middle 1920's. There was this old farm couple that had been married for ages and had about six or eight grown children. The husband was a big fellow, over six feet, five inches tall, and his wife was barely five feet and weighed about 90 pounds. He was basically a good man, who worked hard all week long, causing no problems, but on the weekends he got drunk and verbally abused everybody in his path. This went on for years and years. His wife was very quiet and a strong Christian who went to church every Sunday, but the man didn't attend.

Finally it got to the point where it was very bad. So this particular weekend the man got drunk, went on a rampage and then passed out on the bed into a stupor-induced sleep. Guess this episode was the straw that broke the camel's back, so to speak. As the man was sleeping, his wife got her needle and thread and sewed him up in the bed. She went up between the sheets and sewed the lower and upper sheets together. The old farmer was not aware of what his wife had done, and as he lay sleeping she took a broom handle and whipped him from top to bottom. According to the story, he never took another drink of liquor and started going to church.

Now whenever my mother talks about somebody needing an attitude adjustment she says, "HE'S GOT TO GO TO BED SOMETIME."

Sam

Does This Fig Leaf Make Me Look Fat?

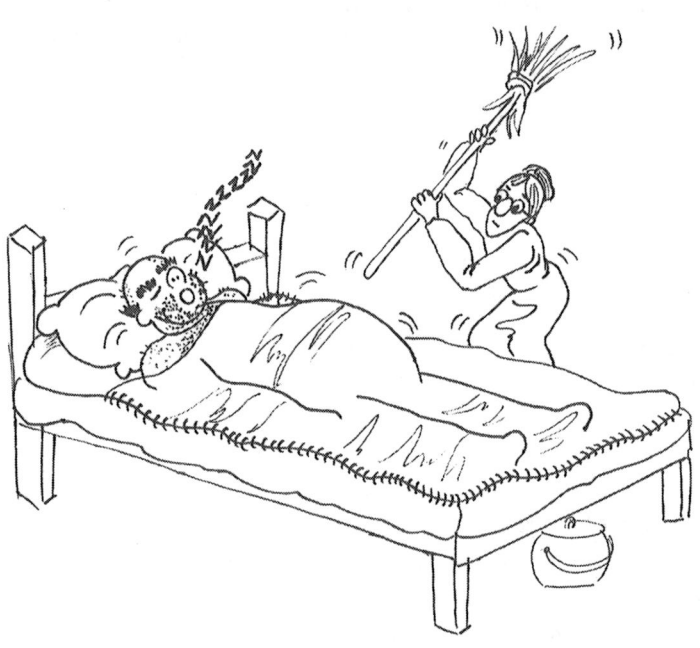

Promises

My husband and I were watching a romantic movie on television and I made a remark to him, "You promised to give me the moon and you haven't." He quickly stood, pulled down his pants and said, "Now, never say I haven't given you the MOON."

Betty

Talking

Most of us are familiar with the idea that, in general, females are more talkative than males. We've also been told that the male-female communication problem exists primarily because women use more words and feeling than men to express themselves in conversation.

My dear hubby and I are no exception to that rule. He's often told people that I was vaccinated with a phonograph needle, and that I'll talk to a signpost and other inanimate objects if humans and pets are not within earshot. I've often told people that I have to pinch him to get him to respond during our conversations.

When asked if I'm always upbeat, laughing and talking about something, he says, "Yep. She's either on or off...and she's only off when she's sleeping. The remote doesn't work on her like it does on the TV, and I have to stay away from her first thing in the morning or she'll chirp me to death."

One night while he was making dinner, I was especially enthusiastic about something and was babbling to him while he was concentrating on fulfilling his personal chef responsibilities for the two of us. I peppered my constant diatribe with questions and finally realized I was being ignored to some degree, when no response was forthcoming. Indignant, I blurted out that he wasn't listening, and what I was saying to him was important to me and could be important for both of us.

He stopped his dicing and chopping and stared at me blankly for a second, then looked sincerely remorseful. He looked at his food project then back at me, shrugged and sadly said, "But, honey, you talk all the time and I can't listen to everything you say...and I can't always tell when what you're going to talk about is important or not."

We looked at each other blankly, then both burst out laughing. When I told a friend about the incident the next *day, she was mortified and asked if I were furious about it. My reply was that there was nothing to be angry about, because he was absolutely right! Since then, I try to remember to announce to my good human sounding board when I am about to utter a statement of importance to merit his attention and response!*

Rosemary

The "Clothes-Horse"

My husband and I have been married forty years and I still haven't accomplished all the changes I've wanted to make in him! So, I just go along with those that irritate me and assume that it's too late to change them.

One change that I've wanted to make is coordinating his clothes. He is definitely not a "clothes-horse." He could care less about buying new shirts, slacks, etc. (I do it for him.) I've had to sneak and throw out old shoes (even a pair that his father wore) and other ancient shirts and pants. Our three grown daughters have tried since their teenage years to teach him about not wearing white socks with dark shoes, and vice-versa. But no such luck, he still does it. So when they see him in his white socks and black sneakers, they automatically say, "Dad, you don't wear so and so together..." and he just smiles and ignores them!

Patty

Heartaches Made Us Closer

In November of last year I had a miscarriage. My husband and I had been trying to get pregnant for a while and it was very stressful and upsetting at first. But I realized it was God's plan and that He was protecting us from something we weren't to know. When I went in for the surgery I had the greatest sense of calm. I believe that I was not only feeling the prayers of others, but that God was truly with me to see me through. We are still trying and I get frustrated sometimes, but it has really brought my husband and myself closer together and strengthened our relationship. I also know the Lord will make it work out exactly how it should.

J'Aimee

Now We Communicate

When my husband became disabled at age 44, role reversals and my husband's lack of self-esteem, etc., caused hardships in our marriage. We talked, but we didn't communicate. His depression and my "need" to save him, to no avail, allowed me to slip into my own depression. I lost my sense of humor and my sense of purpose. I had been "saving" people all of my life and I was failing. Through my own "life saving" therapy, I learned to change my attitude about myself, not about him. I put my wants and needs in the forefront and I became stronger and the laughter returned. I was not trying any more to change him. Something interesting then happened. Once I changed, he changed, too. Now we truly communicate again.

Donna

Quality Time

My uncle had suffered a massive heart attack three years ago. He recovered from it and made a promise to my aunt that they would set aside one day out of the week to spend quality time with each other. So every Wednesday they spend the entire day doing things together. My aunt told me, "This is the closest that we have ever been in our 32 years of marriage."

Janice

Our Closet Date

My husband and I have very hectic schedules. We have four daughters who are all involved in different activities outside of school. We decided to make an effort to spend quality time together every week. We go out on "dates." We enjoy movies, walks on the beach, and my favorite of all is when we sneak off to our bedroom and rendezvous to our secret place—our "walk-in closet." We share special moments reminiscing and laughing about old times, and we talk about growing old together and waiting on the day when the children are all "out of the house!" These special moments bring back those warm, gushy feelings we once felt for one another when we first met!

Janice

The Gifts of Time and Teamwork

There are two married couples I know that really work hard at communication and making their marriage a team. In one couple the dad has a full time job and also runs his own business, and the mother is a stay-at-home mom. He takes off early some days and takes care of their 4 kids for a set block of time for her to have some time for herself. She can use it any way she wishes—read a book, go shopping, day at the spa, lunch or dinner with friends, etc. He deals with all the questions or problems that come up during that time.

The other couple has really worked on communication in their family. The husband and wife set a date night each week. They also set goals for each member of their family, including their three children, to complete. Goals might be: read a book and tell others about it, learn a new skill, a new hobby, and family night (games, movies, etc.). Also they serve together in ministry, helping others as a family. They set boundaries and keep them.

Marcia

CHAPTER FIVE

Fill'er Up Lord... There's a Hole in my Heart Where Hope Used to Be

(Faith)

*"Find rest, O my soul, in God alone;
my hope comes from Him."*
Psalm 62:5

*"Every tomorrow has two handles. We can take hold of it
with the handle of anxiety or the handle of faith."*
Henry Ward Beecher, 19th - century preacher

Life Can be Tough

What is the *worst* stress a human being can experience? Most people start guessing events: a death in the family, divorce, or loss of job. Situations affect people differently. So what is the worst stress? It's a *feeling*, not a situation or event. We are talking about hopelessness, feeling trapped, feeling we have nowhere to turn. Hopelessness is a stronger risk factor for suicidal behavior than depression, according to Dr. Alex Crosby, a medical epidemiologist with the Centers for Disease Control and Prevention.[1]

This is why faith and prayer have to be where we turn first... our foundations for living. Faith may not help us get *around* problems, but it will help us get *through* them. It's very personal and private and each person experiences it in her own way.

Once during a stress management workshop, a participant shared that he used his faith to cope, even at work. Another man, in a very sarcastic tone of voice said, "What does faith have to do with how I do my job?" The first man answered, "Everything." Whether at the workplace or in our personal lives, faith can help us cope with anything. It may not solve all our problems the way we want or take away the sources of the pain and stress, but faith gives us strength to handle them. Faith also gives us hope, and without hope life would have little meaning.

Often people think that if they believe in God, they will be spared pain. God never promised that, and we cannot understand His reasons. Perhaps it is God's way to make us stronger. In the introduction we compared ourselves to the trees. For trees to survive, they need a good root system. But, interestingly enough, trees will not survive and grow without WIND. The very source that can destroy a tree if it is too violent is the same source that gives trees their strength. The movement and swaying of the branches strengthens them to withstand destructive storms. [2] Maybe God allows us to experience trials and hardships to strengthen us like wind strengthens the trees.

"...but we also rejoice in our sufferings, because we know that suffering produces perseverance; perseverance, character; and character, hope. And hope does not disappoint us, because God has poured out His love into our hearts by the Holy Spirit, whom He has given us."
Romans 5:3-5

We can only live our lives a day at a time and trust God. So when I am the main guest at one of my pity parties, I have to remind myself that my life is not just about *me*, and being happy, having fun and getting what I want. Our real reason for being is to serve God, to glorify Him and enjoy Him forever. Turning to God first can then help us manage our stress and our lives in more productive ways, because God wants us to live joyful lives.

Often, however, we slap on a fake smile and suffer inwardly and alone, feeling life has no hope. We may develop the "Why Me?" syndrome and turn to material things, drugs, food or sex to help us cope.

Hurt and pain can send us in two directions. Either we allow our anger at God to drive us further *away* from Him, or our pain sends us *to* Him for comfort and hope. Sometimes it takes pain, and being taken to our knees, to find or grow our faith. And with faith there is hope.

Hope—A Gift From God

One of Linda's favorite analogies about life comes from the eccentric grandmother in the movie *Parenthood*. The family was experiencing the loss of the husband's job, coupled with the surprise news that the wife was expecting their fourth child. Lots of loud, angry barbs were exchanged by the couple, when ole grandma quietly mused:

"You know, when I was nineteen, Grandpa took me on a roller coaster. Up, down, up, down. Oh, what a ride! I always wanted to go again. You know, it was just so interesting to me that a ride could make me so frightened, so scared, so sick, so excited, and so thrilled all together! Some didn't like it. They went on the merry-go-round. It just goes around. Nothing. I like the roller coaster. You get more out of it."

What Linda says she loves most about that quote is that it brings home to her the truth that circumstances *do* change.

We just have to find something secure to hang onto until we crest the hill and experience the thrill. That "something secure" is hope in the Lord.

According to Linda, the roughest roller coaster ride she ever experienced was in 1997.

I was awakened in the middle of the night by the smell of pizza wafting down the hall from our den. I jumped up to see what was going on and discovered that our two sons had decided to make them a late-night snack. Since only one son was in the den, I wandered around trying to locate the other one. I found my 17-year-old standing in front of the mirror in his bathroom looking at a swollen place on his neck. I felt it and immediately experienced "Mom panic." Had it not been one o'clock in the morning, I would have had the doctor on the phone in a flash. Needless to say, next morning we were on the way to the pediatrician with the first available appointment. That was the beginning of our roller coaster ride. What was diagnosed as probable mononucleosis never manifested itself, so Mom had him back to the doctor within a week. After more tests showing nothing new and assurances that it was probably nothing, we went home to "watch" the knot that never did go away. So, good ole Mom called the doctor again and we were referred—as a precaution—to a surgeon and an oncologist for a biopsy. Two words you never want to hear in the same sentence are oncologist and your child's name. Hard-core panic was beginning to set in.

What began as probable mono ended up being Hodgkin's disease, a cancer of the lymph system. I will never forget the doctor's comment when he explained the illness and the treatment to my husband and myself. He said, 'You look like you have been hit by a Mack Truck.' Couldn't have described us better myself. Then he said, 'In a few months, you will look very different. This is highly curable...it will just be a blip on his screen of life.' Even though that doctor was thankfully proven to be exactly right, what I don't think he understood was that I didn't want my son to just be better in a few months. I WANTED THIS NEVER TO HAVE HAPPENED AT ALL! I didn't want to learn any valuable life lessons that could make my family stronger. I just wanted it to go away.

So, I turned to the Lord. I prayed earnestly for him to give me the cancer instead of my son. Then, when I began feeling sick and running a fever, I panicked and thought the Lord had answered my prayer! What I really meant was for neither one of us to have cancer, Lord! The truth was that I became ill because my inner resources were drained from stress, panic, and trying so hard to control everything. I knew from my faith that I needed to place my son in the Lord's hands and leave him there. But I couldn't be sure that what the Lord had planned for him fit exactly with I wanted to have happen. I searched the scriptures for guidance. A friend asked me if I had experienced God's peace about the situation, and I had to admit that I hadn't. Then I found this verse that enabled me to turn my son back over to the Lord and experience the rest and peace that freed me up to be strong for him through his chemotherapy and full recovery process: 'For I know the plans I have for you, declares the Lord. Plans to prosper you and not to harm you, plans to give you hope and a future.' Jeremiah 29:11

I must admit that every time we approached a CT scan, pulmonary test, or one of the many other checks they performed on him during his treatment and follow up, my old demons would rear their ugly heads and cause tightening in my gut. Being grounded in God's sovereignty brought us safely through that roller coaster ride and, amazingly, left us more prepared for other rides on other roller coasters that were to come!

Charles Swindol, Christian pastor, author and speaker, explains hope in a way everyone can understand. He says,

"Hope is a wonderful gift from God, a source of strength and courage in the face of life's harshest trials." He points out that when we are discouraged, hope can lift us up. When we want to give up, hope can keep us going. When we feel the future is dark, hope gives us light.[3]

It's so interesting to me how God sends messages of hope when we really need them. There was a time in my life I was feeling stressed, hopeless and down, because I couldn't see any relief or solution to my problems. The very next Sunday my minister preached a sermon about how even Christians can feel forsaken by God. My ears perked up because, to be honest, that was exactly how I was feeling at the moment. He talked about God's love and then pointed out three things I really needed to hear. First, when faced with overwhelming problems, we tend to start generalizing—everything is bad, nothing is going right, nobody cares! Second, this problem will last forever! Third, this problem happens only to me and no one understands! Of course, none of those are true. Not *everything* is bad and *some* people do care. The problem will not last forever—*everything changes*, good and bad. An old saying applies here—*this too shall pass*!

There was a situation once during one of my classes where a woman just sat there, didn't participate or speak and seemed very nonchalant. I remember thinking that she must not like the class. After the seminar another woman told me that the woman had said to her, "There is no hope or solution to my problem; everyday I wake up and decide whether this is the day I will commit suicide. My Christian faith is the only thing holding me back." I related this incident to another group the next day and asked them their opinion of what I should do. A woman came up and said, "Go to her, she needs your strength—and she needs hope." She told me she was in a similar position once—dealing with problems with her son and feeling frustrated and hopeless, but her friends at work took charge and got her help.

One instance in particular of faith and hope stands out in my mind. My father had his first heart attack at the age of forty-one and almost died. He recovered, but spent the next twenty years of his life in and out of hospitals, fighting cancer and heart problems. Even with all he went through, my father was a positive, upbeat person and a very strong Christian. He taught me so much about faith and hope. During one round of hospitalization he went into cardiac arrest and was technically dead for two minutes before being revived. After he came home, I asked him about his experience and he became very quiet and pensive. What he shared with me calmed my fears and doubts about death and dying and truly strengthened my faith. My father was a quiet man, but once he started telling me his story, his words just flowed. He told me he had experienced a feeling of peace and joy like he had never felt in his entire life. What he remembered were bright lights at the end of a tunnel and a warm sensation of being pulled toward the lights. He told me he wanted to go with all his heart. Then, all of a sudden, he was being pulled back from the lights and was angry because he didn't want to come back. Later, as books on near-death experiences were published, they gave almost identical descriptions. But my father's experience was before any of those books were published! He told me he had never feared death, but was grateful he had been given more time, since he was not ready to leave his family yet. However, more than ever, he knew death was just the beginning. The unknown is frightening for most of us and his experience strengthened my faith and renewed my hope as a Christian.

Faith and Hope Stories

The Path to Peace

Jim and I moved to the Presbyterian Home so that our children would no longer have to worry about our daily needs. It was our gift to them.

Two months later, Jim suffered a fatal stroke—a violent end to a relationship of sixty-one glorious years.

My security was threatened. I was dismayed and not ready to give up our cherished bond of love and devotion. I was in denial and disbelief. Why did this have to happen when we had reached that lofty privileged plateau of love, joy and peace?

We had often discussed the fact that our time together was limited with our 87 and 85 years. But I did not want it to happen this way. We needed more time.

Of course, we were a normal couple who had overcome the usual problems and pains as parents. We enjoyed deep fellowship with our two endearing daughters.

I was overwhelmed—I struggled—I prayed. I refused to feel sorry for myself as I knew that millions had experienced the same and even worse losses than mine.

My Presbyterian faith was tested. I asked God for help and finally accepted His comfort. It has been said that there is a blessing sent from God in every burden of sorrow and that faith can draw the sting out of every trouble. But where was that blessing...the sting was still there. I had been blessed and it was up to me to change my outlook and my attitude. I should be grateful.

When I realized that death is God's final healing touch and that Jim was healed and at rest, I resigned to the future. Death has no tongue—neither did I. I did not want to discuss my situation nor my future.

Friends here at Presbyterian Home were instantly so special in their depth of love, concern and friendship. They became my family. Even a warm handshake added an extra *dimension of kindness and sympathy. The silent beauty of flowers that were sent was almost an embrace expressing admiration to one who had been so highly esteemed. All of that strengthened my faith in God and my trust in mankind.*

Gradually I became aware of the fact that life must go on and that there was willing support from friends and loved ones. My gratitude for God's blessings brought a smile in my heart and friends doubled my meager happiness as they shared my grief.

I could go on. I am grateful. My life now is one of contentment. I am very humble as I realize that God has always guided my life and has given me more blessings than I deserve. I have found peace.

Name Withheld

My Special Reason

When I was a teenager I went through a period of depression. My mother, a very dear and wise person, gave me a great deal of attention and love. One day she told me something about my past that made a lasting impression. She told me that before I was born my oldest brother was very ill. The doctors, when she told them she was pregnant, told her she could not go through a pregnancy because she was so weak and run down. They said she should end the pregnancy. She said after much thought and prayer she could not agree—so I was born. My brother recovered. I've always felt I must be here for some special reason. I've never felt that I know of any special instance in my life that is outstanding, but I feel that being here at the Presbyterian Home gives me a chance everyday to do my best to find out.

Name Withheld

Grace and Peace

I remember in college I went through a very difficult summer. I spent a month crying—everyday. It was severe depression. I called my mom, but she could not fix the hurt. She sent my sisters to stay with me, thinking that perhaps I was just homesick. But, neither did that solve the problem. Day after day, I woke up gripped with fear and panic—then tears.

That summer, I was working as an intern in the public relations department of Mercy Hospital in Des Moines. Each day, as I drove the 45-minute commute from Ames, I would concoct the headlines of my death... "ISU student dies in fiery crash in cornfield"...the details of the story would describe my depression and unveil that the probable cause was tear-blurred vision.

Each Tuesday was "dark room day." I spent the entire day in the dark room, developing pictures that I had taken throughout the week of various hospital events. It was also a time when I could let down the mask I bravely put on for my co-workers, and I could cry all day long. Looking back, I realize that it was no coincidence that the only radio station I could receive was an AM Christian talk station! God used that venue to communicate His love to me through His only Son, who died that I could have joy, even here in this troubled world.

One day, as I passed the hospital chapel, I was drawn inside. I flipped through the songbook, and I found the hymn—"On Eagle's Wings"—I started singing (yes, by myself!) the words... "And He will raise you up on eagle's wings, Bear you on the breath of dawn, Make you to shine like the sun, and Hold you in the palm of His hand." I sang those words over and over. And then I cried out to Him. And He answered. When I left that chapel, I was free from the *crying and the depression. I knew that God was holding me in the palm of His hand.*

Since that day, my life has been a progression toward Him. Some days are easier than others. There are things that happen in this world that break my heart and boggle my mind—tragedies such as 9/11 or the loss of a child, like my sweet cousin Rachel, who died from cancer at the age of 8. Some things I recognize are brought on by the sinfulness of man. Others leave me perplexed. But, I know from studying His Word that He will never leave or forsake me. I know that He works ALL things together for the good of those who love Him and who are called, according to His purpose. He sent His ONLY Son to die—a sacrifice beyond comprehension—so that we could have life eternal. This is what I CLING to when the world gets crazy. For this world is not the best He has to offer! I know, some would question how a God who loves us this much, could allow us to suffer through the travesties of this life. Forced love is not pleasurable. If you had to force your spouse to marry you at gunpoint, it would lack the JOY of someone loving you whole-heartedly and willingly. God doesn't want to force us. Instead, He sent a message that says—"here's how much I love you! I will sacrifice my beloved Son so that you can have the righteousness needed to live in Heaven and eternity with me always. Please accept my gift."

Jesus said that there were two great commandments. The first, to love God with all your heart, and all your soul, and all your mind. The second is to love your neighbor as you would yourself. Later, He gives another commandment—that we would love one another, just as He has loved us. This is sacrificial love—love that is willing to go to a cross. You see, God does not promise a trouble-free life, but He does promise comfort when trouble comes. Sometimes this comfort comes from someone who has been through a similar situation—and who is now able to provide empathy. Sometimes it comes through His Word. This is contrary to worldly thinking that says, "Look out for yourself. You are more important that anyone else is. Make sure you take care of you—and then, if there's anything left—sure, help out those people you like."

I have found that I may not always understand (and there are lots of things that I don't) –He is unchanging, wholly loving and is not capable of lying. Therefore, I can trust that if His Word says that He is working all things together for the good of those who love Him, HE IS. It is when I don't understand that I realize that I am probably focused in on a thread—and He is looking at the overall tapestry of life.

Andrea

Faith and Hope Are All I've Got

After crying all morning I finally pulled myself out of my bed and started thinking again about my daughter. Allie is seventeen years old and trying her best to self-destruct—drinking, drugs, sex, flunking out of high school, no regard for self or others. When you're a mother and love your daughter dearly it breaks your heart to see your child on a dead-end road. What stress and what an out of control feeling when nothing you do seems to help. Today was a roller coaster of feelings. First there was anger, then depression. A sense of hopelessness just washed over me and I felt paralyzed, and the rest of the day felt like I was just going through the motions of living. As night came I started talking to God, asking Him for strength to go on. At first I admit I felt almost angry and that what I was doing was a waste of time. Then as I continued talking, a certain peace came over me—God was telling me to have faith and hand it all over to Him and peace would come to me. It's sometimes so difficult to let go and trust God.

Name Withheld

I Am a Miracle of God's Grace

My mother is one of four sisters. She has one brother whom she has had no contact with for forty years. She and her sisters never speak except to be cruel to each other. When one died recently my mother didn't attend the funeral—she was still trying to prove her point about what an awful person her sister was. My mother has been married four times. Her first husband and she were divorced after they got into a fight and one (or both) of them drank rat poison. My father and she were married almost ten years. I was six and my brother was two when they divorced. My father stayed in Libya and my mother brought us back to the US, so I saw my father about six more times during my growing up years. This left us, by brother and me, totally in the care of someone who was mentally ill and physically and emotionally abusive.

My mother was institutionalized twice for "nervous breakdowns" for periods of up to a year when I was in elementary school, leaving me and my brother in the care of her older sister. My mother attempted suicide twice before I was ten years old. By age fourteen, I was in foster care and glad to be there. I have one cousin in Folsom prison for a double homicide. My other cousins are unmarried. Two of them have mental problems and histories of substance abuse. Both are unable to hold down jobs. Another cousin is forty and lives with his mother, and works as a janitor at the local high school. My brother has been married many times (I don't know the exact number), and the woman he lives with now is not his wife. He is forty-five.

My life is a testament to God's grace. There is no other explanation why I should have been spared the lives of my relatives. Yet I have been married for thirty years to someone who still loves me! I have three children who are successful in their education and career choices, who are well adjusted and who have never been in trouble with drugs or alcohol. I *own a successful business, and I earn a good living. I have a home; a refuge and sanctuary from the world. A home and family I love and where I am loved.*

My life is a living testimony to the fact that God can choose to turn around a life. God can choose to break the cycle. God reveals Himself to those whom He will, and He enables us to respond to His grace in a manner that is honoring to Him. There is no other explanation for my life. To those who say I overcame difficult circumstances I say, why me? Why not my cousins? Why not my brother? It is supreme arrogance for me to say that I did this on my own. It can be nothing other than the hand of God. God called me out of the darkness of this world, and showed me his love and grace. He gave me the Holy Spirit, which has guided my response to Him, and enlightened me about heavenly things and His word. He showed me the way of salvation through His son, Jesus Christ, and all I had to do was to keep my heart open. What amazing good news that is for each and every one of us. God picks us up and holds us in the palm of His hand, in His tender care and mercy.

Lyn

My Thorn

I was born with what the doctor's (for lack of a better diagnosis) called left spastic hemeplesia ("mild Cerebral Palsy") on my left side. Not enough to use a wheelchair or a brace but enough to trip over my own feet and make life very interesting. I am a half a twitcher. I know that life can be funny and my husband thinks it's "very interesting." For example, have you ever carried two cups of coffee at one time? I can too, one real and one imaginary. My right hand carries the real one and my left is hooked into the invisible one. Have you ever jumped out of your skin at a scary movie? I jump out of only half of my skin. It takes only half the time to calm down again. With most people it takes two hands to type 40 words per minute. I can type 35 with one. You try it.

All in all I am truly known as a naturally born klutz. I have accomplished more than I ever was expected to and I thank God everyday that he gave me this thorn. It gives me a chance to show many people that no matter what, everyone can be useful. Handicapped doesn't mean that our brain doesn't work and it has taught me not to give up without a fight and always have hope.

Marjorie

Hope

When I look back over this past year of my life, never thinking for once I would be diagnosed with breast cancer, I realize it has made me go back and look at my entire life and understand now that God was putting me in this direction everyday. I grew up with an alcoholic father and lived in a very abusive lifestyle the first nine years of my life. My father did not abuse the children, but abused my mother, and finally they divorced when I was nine. My mother died when I was fourteen, my father died when I was sixteen. I think as a teenager you are very resilient and that resiliency brought me through their deaths, but at the same time made me a more compassionate person and led me to my career in nursing. You know, thinking back, I knew before I even graduated from nursing school that cancer would be the area that I would want to specialize in. I remember coming to Lexington Medical Center with one year left in Nursing School, and felt I needed to work as a nurse tech to get some experience. I went in to Human Resources and gave them my application. The recruiter asked what area I wanted to work in and I told her I wanted to work sixteen hours a week and had always felt drawn to work in Oncology. She looked at me funny and said that is exactly the area we have an opening. That led me to the Oncology floor and I absolutely fell in love with the patients. Through the last ten years I have developed wonderful relationships with these patients, many of whom are now deceased. I realize that I am so much the better person because they were a part of my life and they have also helped shape me into the person that I am. Then I was diagnosed with cancer. Having worked with cancer patients on a daily basis, I realized how short life is and figured out what the important things in life are. Some people say that life after cancer is better, but I feel that my life was as good before as post cancer. What is better is that I *was able to, for the first time in my life, totally submit myself to God. I was one of those people that always liked to do it MYSELF and had never done a very good job of 100% giving it to God and letting Him take care of it. That's one thing that cancer taught me, that I had to just hand it to the Lord and that He would take care of me. I tell people everywhere that I just can't describe the peace He gave me during my diagnosis and treatment. I have been so blessed by the friends He surrounded me with. I have truly just said, "Lord whatever happens, it's yours, You will take care of me," and that's exactly how I plan to live my life. Not just about the cancer, either, with the everyday things, the small things. I try to go over to the hospital everyday and walk the stairs. I pray all the way that the Lord will get me up these ten flights of stairs! I look at my life as a whole and know that I have been tested in so many ways. I could be such a pathetic, bitter person right now if I chose to, but I have made the decision that I don't want to live my life that way. I catch myself looking at people and thinking, gosh these people have had such easy lives, what makes them so different from me? What I have realized over the last year of my life is that I'm so much better because of the struggles that I've gone through. It means so much at the end of the day that I lay my head down on the pillow and feel the peace of God in my heart.*

Kelly

Prayer

At the age of seventeen years old I went to high school and worked part time at a store. One Saturday after work I was driving home and had a head-on car accident. The other person was reaching in her floorboard to get something. After the collision I remained conscious and started to pray. I prayed to God to help me; I wasn't ready to die. I was trapped in the car and had broken ribs and internal bleeding. I had busted out the windshield with my face and broke my arm and leg. When the rescue department got to me they said they would get me out and I'd be fine. I went to the hospital and had two surgeries and many blood transfusions and also had to have surgery on my ankle. I was told I could have bled to death in three minutes but somehow the injury clotted itself. The doctor said I was the youngest person to live through the first surgery, much less the second one. I remember everything and am blessed to be alive. The other person died three hours after the accident. I spent eight days in intensive care and seven days in a regular room. Three weeks after the accident I graduated from Lake City High School in a wheel chair. I spent three months in that wheel chair and walked with a limp for a while. I know that God came to me that day and saved my life. I am now thirty-three years old, have a thirteen-year-old son and life is good.

Deanna

God Provides

Over the last few years my eyes have been opened to many of the blessings God has given me. I'm not saying I always get what I want, but God always provides what I need when I need it.

I have been blessed with a loving, kind and supportive husband. He is evidence that God does answer prayers! I am also blessed with friendships. I have friends who have prayed for a "hedge" of protection through difficult times. It is great to have people around who are willing to share in the good and bad times.

My parents separated in 2002. It was something that I saw coming but was smart enough to know it would be the start of a long, hard road. My dad called me the Sunday my mom left and told me he was happier than he had been in years. That was a short-lived emotion. He tried to commit suicide three days later by overdosing on his medication. When my husband and I got him in the car and on the way to the hospital to have his stomach pumped, he said he would never forgive me. I went through several months of dreading the telephone or door bell ringing...I was on a roller coaster with my dad...one phone call was letting me hold it for things I had absolutely no control over...the next phone call may be an apology. I finally got to a point where I had to stand up for myself and tell him that he was my father and I love him, but I also love my mom. The relationship was on occasion abusive, and my mom needed to get out. I would have probably left years before she did. As a result of the separation and divorce, I don't have a relationship with my dad. It was not by my choice, but I do believe it is for the best, as I have spent countless hours in prayer over this. My husband and I were going through Rick Warren's **The Purpose Driven Life**, and I began to have doubts if I had done all I was supposed to do biblically. Re-assured, I tried to talk with my dad...my husband and I tried to talk with my dad…my pastor talked with my dad. God has given me a peace about my dad's decision. Maybe when his anger goes away, he will find himself in a position to want to be my dad again. But there is great comfort in knowing that I have a Father in heaven who has never closed the door on me.

I know this will sound really out there, but early in their separation I had a strange dream one night. I dreamed I was in my backyard. My dog kept going from one side of our yard to the other barking. I went out to check on her, and realized our neighbors had company. I tried quieting her down but was unsuccessful. Then out of the corner of my eye I saw the most demonic creature I could imagine. All of a sudden I was fighting with this creature. Even though we were in battle, I realized he could not touch me…all of a sudden I woke up. God had spoken to me…it was absolutely clear that evil could not touch me…I am protected from the evil one. Times may be tough, but I know who is in control.

Today even as another part of my family is going through another break-up, and Brad and I are waiting on an answer to our prayer as to whether or not to adopt a child, we know that God has our best intentions at heart and will lead us down the right path. For now we will continue to live the "good life"…we'll do our best to "act justly, love mercy and walk humbly."

Name Withheld

The Good Samaritan

This story really happened, and it renewed my faith in people as well as my faith in God.

My background is in sales and I was on my way to an interview for a sales position that is available within the company that I currently work for. Now, there are two things in life that I love with a passion. Of course I adore my two children, Dillon who is ten, and Blair who is two, and my family. But in addition to them, the top two are working in a sales position and the beach. Here I am on my way to an interview for a sales job that is located in Myrtle Beach. Talk about anxious, nervous and excited! To add to my emotions....my gas hand is below "E" and the gaslight has been on. My checking account is overdrawn, and I honestly had $2.00 and some change with me. So, in addition to praying for God to help me do my best with this interview, I am praying to be able to have enough gas to even get there. Okay, I made it to the interview, and felt comfortable with the way that it went (thank you God)...But I still had this gas hand on empty to deal with. Luckily, there were two gas stations within about a mile. There was one on the right, and one on the left. I am driving down the right hand side praying that I make it to the gas station. For some reason, I do not choose the gas station on the right which would have been easier, but get in the "turning lane" to cross the road and go to the gas station on the left. I pull up to the pump, walk inside and ask the cashier if they took checks. IF they did, I would make a mad rush home and roll pennies or whatever I had to do to get money in to cover the check. The cashier advised me that they didn't accept checks, so I told her to give me just a minute, and I got my $2.00 out, and was digging for loose change. A man, who was standing over to the side waiting to pay for his purchase, handed the cashier a $5.00 bill for me to use for gas. I thanked him and told him that I just couldn't accept. He *continued to insist that I take it and put $7.00 worth of gas in my minivan instead of $2.00. He asked me where I had to go and I answered, home at Lake Murray (which was about 45 miles away). When the man heard this he absolutely insisted that I use the $5.00 for gas. I wanted to hug him I was so grateful. But instead, I just thanked him and thanked him. I told him he was my blessing and an answered prayer! He is the reason that I made it home to my two boys. Now I know why I went to the gas station on the left...there was an Angel and a Blessing waiting for me. I am 35 years old, the mother of two boys, I work full time and there are daily things that I deal with that I feel I just can't "handle" anymore. I have realized that I don't have to handle things by myself; God will help you with the burden if you ask Him to and let Him. I have put my faith in God and have asked him to lead me where He thinks I should be...and I'll have to get back to you about my interview! I have put that in God's hands as well.*

Kathy

Thankful for my "Fleas"

For the last 9 years, I have kept a Gratitude Journal. Every night I write down at least 5 things that happened that day that I am grateful for. This is not an original idea—I'm sure many people do it.

At the end of my list, when circumstances warrant, I add any "Fleas" that might have occurred during the day. I got the term from Corrie Ten Boom's book, **The Hiding Place**.

In her story, Corrie tells of the time she and her sister, Betsie, were moved into Barracks 28 at the Ravensbruck Concentration Camp. It was full of fleas. That first night, as they said their prayers, Betsie added: "Thank you, God, for the fleas." Corrie was horrified. Those fleas were nothing but horrid pests that bit and invaded the bedding. Corrie said she could not bring herself to thank God for the fleas. But Betsie reminded her about what they had recently read in First Thessalonians: "Rejoice always, pray constantly, give thanks in all circumstances..." They must thank God for all things.

It was the sisters' custom to conduct evening Bible Study wherever they were. At all the other camps and barracks, the Bible Study was soon broken up by the cruel guard who allowed nothing of the kind. However, this particular Bible Study grew and grew, with many women coming to know Jesus Christ.

Some time later, a woman in their barracks died and the ladies were told to take the body outside. These women were weak and malnourished and not used to having to move the bodies of the dead. When they asked the matron why the guards did not come and get it themselves (the usual practice), they were told the guards refused to enter the flea-ridden barracks. Hence, the Bible Study had grown and grown without their interference.

So, when there are negative things that happen in my day, things that I have a very hard time thanking God for, I try to remember to 'thank God for all things' and I write them down as "Fleas." I often see where good things came about because of that particular piece of negativity. A piece of negativity I might not have remembered, if I had not written it down and been able to follow the miraculous work of God.

"In all things, give thanks."

Pat

CHAPTER SIX

Put on That Red Dress… and Go to the Party

(Really *Living* Your Life)

Epitaph… died age 40, buried age 60. Have you ever known someone like that? They have been "dead" for 20 years and didn't even know it. They are biologically alive, but emotionally and spiritually dead. God gives us one life on this earth. It's our way of getting ready to meet Him. He wants us to live life… not just exist. God did not promise a life without problems. There will be stress, divorces, financial problems, heartaches and health problems. He did promise us He would be there to help us along the way. There is a Danish proverb that says, *"What you are is God's gift to you; what you do with yourself is your gift to God."*

My stepdaughter, Amy, is a great example of that quote:
   Hi! My name is Amy. I feel very lucky to be alive, since at the age of 9, I came close to not living at all. You see I was in a life- threatening wreck, had severe head injuries, and was in a coma for over 2 months. The doctors said I probably would not live. Boy, did I prove them wrong! You

see, I was determined I wasn't ready to give up yet. God had given me another chance but I didn't really know why. When I woke from the coma, the doctors told my parents there was a good chance, due to the extensive head injuries, I might never walk again. Well, I now work in the medical profession as an occupational therapy assistant, where I am on my feet all day. I proved them wrong again.

    I started back to school 6 months after the wreck. It wasn't easy, but like they say "life never is." When I started back, I was in the fifth grade and I went from riding in a wheelchair to using a walker to finally walking on my own. The thing I hated most about the wheelchair was the way people would look at you like something was wrong. For years after my wreck I felt sorry for myself, poor me. My life would never be the same. Then one day I realized the world was not going to stop for me. And no matter how people looked at me, they were really concerned with themselves, not me. So you see, I wasted all those years and all that energy feeling sorry for myself.

    After high school, I started to volunteer at different hospitals and other organizations. I saw lots of people who were in worse shape than me. I wanted to help them, and I thought maybe this is why God saved my life, so that I could give back. I started to work with kids with special needs, which is a challenge in itself.

    I have had a few setbacks, like a few parents not wanting me to treat their kids because of some physical challenges I still have. My balance is not 100%, and I cannot use the right side of my body well because of the lasting brain injury. My voice is sometimes raspy because, when they put in the trachea tube to help me breathe, my vocal cords were punctured. It hurts when people have that kind of attitude and I did cry a little. But you got to think out of the five that don't want you, there are five hundred who do.

My recovery was not short. It took many years and lots of hard work and definitely wasn't easy. There will always be a part of me that wishes it never happened to me. But it made me who I am today, a young woman given another chance at life by God. And I feel God wants me to use my compassion and understanding to help children with brain injuries learn to live their lives the best they can. So when kids say to me, "You just don't understand." I say, "Oh, yes I do, and if I can do it, so can you!"

We cannot wait for problems to go away. Really *living* is about squeezing joy out of life in the midst of problems... and really looking for joy. I remember a day one summer walking down to our garden with my husband and five-year-old grandson, Alex. It had not been a good day and, I'll admit, I wasn't particularly joyful at the time. Alex turned to my husband and asked, "Pop, do you grow hamburgers?" I burst out laughing and my bad mood just evaporated.

Many people keep journals and diaries as a way of handling stress. A woman once told me she kept a journal for years. However, one day she realized that all she ever wrote in the journal were the negative things that had happened to her. So she decided to change her focus and started keeping a gratitude journal. Each night she would write down all the things she was grateful for on that day. It might be seeing an old friend, the opportunity for helping someone or having a great laugh. How often do we only focus on the negatives?

As we have written this book, Linda says she has found herself repeatedly singing the old song, "Looking for Love in All the Wrong Places." Since the beginning of time, many women have been doing just that. We worry that we are not good enough, pretty enough, smart enough, happy enough, rich enough, accepted enough and on and on. We're like the tree mentioned earlier in this book, jerked back and forth and eventually uprooted by the winds of circumstance, doubt, insecurity, fear, and others' opinions. Only when our self-worth is grounded in faith in the one who loves us UNCONDITIONALLY are we able to accept ourselves and grow to be who He intended us to be. Like Eve in the Garden of Eden, we get to *choose* how we will respond in the face of difficult circumstances. A cancer support group member shared this humorous story that illustrates that point:

A cousin of mine, after experiencing a very disgraceful and embarrassing situation, was trying to put her life back together again. I called to offer her my support, not knowing what to say. So I told her exactly that. I was sorry this had happened and I didn't know what in the world to say that would help. Her reply was— "Yes, it's awful, but all I can do is put on my red dress and go to the party!" That has become my motto, and may I say that I have almost worn out my red dress.

So, really LIVE your life. Put on that red dress... or fig leaf... and go to the party!

Notes

Chapter 1 Don't Look Now, But Your Attitude is Showing

1. Barbara Johnson, *Splashes of Joy in the Cesspools of Life* (Dallas, Texas: Word Publishing, 1992), page 65.
2. Mary E. Frye, poem *Do Not Stand at my Grave and Weep*, published as a poem to comfort a bereaved friend.
3. Ella Wheeler Wilcox, "The Winds of Fate," *The Best Loved Poems of the American People*, compiled by Hazel Felleman (Garden City, N.Y.: Garden City Books, 1936), page 364.
4. Donald B. Ardell, *High Level Wellness* (Emmaus PA, Rodale Press), page 145.

Chapter 2 Laughter—Joy in the Middle of Junk

1. Charles Swindol, *Laugh Again* (Dallas, Texas: Word Publishing, 1992), page 20.
2. Poem, "A Beautiful Prayer," Source unknown.
3. Source Unknown.

Chapter 3 Feeling Like a Raggedy Ann in a Barbie World

1. Barbara Johnson, *Stick a Geranium in Your Hat and Be Happy* (Dallas, Texas: Word Publishing, 1990), page 140.
2. Maxwell Maltz, M.D., *The Magic Power of Self-Image Psychology* (New York, Pocket Books, 1970), Introduction.
3. Dr. Alexander Leaf, "Every Day is a Gift When You Are Over 100," *National Geographic*, January, 1973, pages 93-118.
4. Poem, "I'm Fine," Source Unknown.
5. Floyd and Eve Corbin, *How to Relax in a Busy World* (Prenctice Hall 1962).
6. Poem, "The Girls," used with permission by Margie Tolly.
7. www.thinkExists.com, quotations online, 1 August 2011.

Chapter 4 And Adam Said, "Eve, Honey, Have You Seen My Rib?"

1. WWW.JOKESPLUS.COM.
2. Walter Wangerin, Jr., *As For Me and My House* (Nashville, Thomas Nelson Publishers, 1990), page 82.
3. Judith Wallerstein and Sandra Blakeslee, *Good Marriage* (Grand Central Publishing, N.Y., 1995).
4. Phyllis Diller, *Phyllis Diller's Housekeeping Hints*, 1966.
5. Lewis B. Smeades, *Forgive and Forget: Healing the Hurts We Don't Deserve* (San Francisco: Harper and Row, 1984), page 21.

Chapter 5 Fill'er Up, Lord.... There's a Hole in My Heart Where Hope Used to Be

1. Dr. Alex Crosby, medical epidemiologist, Centers for Disease Control and Prevention, article from *The State* Newspaper, a Knight Ridder Company, March 19, 2005.
2. Biosphere 2 Experiment, see John Polk Allen.
3. Charles Swindol, *Hope Again* (W Publishing Group, 1996), page xi, xii.

For more information about purchasing books or scheduling Merry Taylor or Linda Sloan for speaking engagements, contact them at:

Taylor and Associates
803-622-3161
taylorandassoc@sc.rr.com

Please visit our website at
www.taylorandassoc.com

CPSIA information can be obtained at www.ICGtesting.com
Printed in the USA
LVOW121042040112
262363LV00001B/3/P